HEAR US ROAR!

By

The Teen Writers Guild of Lindenwold High School

Bloomington, IN   authorHOUSE®   Milton Keynes, UK

AuthorHouse™
1663 Liberty Drive, Suite 200
Bloomington, IN 47403
www.authorhouse.com
Phone: 1-800-839-8640

AuthorHouse™ UK Ltd.
500 Avebury Boulevard
Central Milton Keynes, MK9 2BE
www.authorhouse.co.uk
Phone: 08001974150

First published by AuthorHouse 1/16/2007

ISBN: 978-1-4259-8727-5 (sc)

Printed in the United States of America
Bloomington, Indiana

This book is printed on acid-free paper.

Cover design credits: Tara Ringenwald and Lisabeth Carl
Photo Credits: Leslie Betts-Woodward
Ms. Kristen's photo by Jonathan Reed-West
End quote: Forest Witcraft

Dedication

To the Future Members of
The Teen Writers Guild of
Lindenwold High School

All men and women are born, live, suffer and die -- what distinguishes us one from another is our dreams, whether they be dreams about worldly or unworldly things, and what we do to make them come about...

We do not choose to be born.

We do not choose our parents.

We do not choose our historical epoch, the country of our birth, or the immediate circumstances of our upbringing.

We do not, most of us, choose to die; nor do we choose the time and conditions of our death.

But within this realm of choicelessness…

We do choose how we live.

- Joseph Epstein

Founding Guild Members
2006

Brittany Alston

Lessy Bonilla

Amara Bowen

Ian Brown

Vanessa Brown

Lisabeth Carl

Diana Casas

Francisco Colon

Makepeace Cotto

Lisa Curcio

Rob Di Clementi

Gregory Forest

Desiree Forrest

Tyree Frierson

Bonvincent Hernandez

Megan Herrera

Jessica Kealey

Anna Kriner

Melinda Lee

Michael Lipshultz

Antione McGee

David N. Megginson

Sarafina Muhammad

Caitlin Mullaney

Madalyn Natividad

Bhagyesh Nayi

Abrianna Wilp-O'Neill

Victor Palillero

Danielle Palombo

Ivan A. Pineiro

Cynthia Recarte

Britt Robertson

Symone Robinson

Yeni Rodriguez

Ariana Ross

Brionna Scotton

Karla Siete

Makeda Robinson-Smalls

Tashae Smith

Dana Terry

Briana A. Woodruff

Acknowledgments

From Brittany Alston:
First and foremost, I must give honor and thanks to my Lord and Savior, for He makes all things possible. I also want to thank my wonderful mother and father. They have given me so many opportunities to grow into the person I am proud to be. I also want to thank my family and church family for all of their love, prayers, and support. I would like to say thank you to my best friend Leah, and all of my friends for their encouragement. Last but not least, I want to give a huge thank you to Judith Kristen for this amazing opportunity! She has no idea how grateful I am to be part of this wonderful project!

From Lessy Bonilla
First, I give thanks to God for letting me write these poems. Also, I am glad that my parents have always been there for me. I dedicate these poems to them, and to my brothers and sisters. They are all I have. I love you guys! Oh, and how I can forget my ESL teacher and ...?

From Amara Bowen:
First and foremost, I would like to thank Matthew Regulas for inspiring all of my work. I would also like to thank my family for always supporting what I do, and last, but certainly not least, I would like to thank my three best friends: Symone, Dana, and Tiffy for always being there for me.

From Ian Brown:
There are many people and things that inspired me to write all of the poems that I have written. I would like to thank my mother, my father and my entire family. This might seem a bit strange, but I would like to thank the bad times. I don't want anymore of them but the bad times inspired me to write many of my poems. Most of all, I would love to thank the person who made all of this happen, Ms. Judith

Kristen. She got me motivated, and this could launch my writing career, all thanks to her.

Thank you to everyone involved, especially Ms. Kristen, for this opportunity.

From Vanessa Brown:

I would like to thank first and foremost, God! I also want to thank my mother, who is always my inspiration And, BIG love and thanks also to my Dad my two sisters, my three brothers, and all of my family and friends, *and* my English teacher, Ms. Ryan. For anyone else who I might have omitted, please charge it to my mind and not to my heart.

From Lizabeth Carl/Luna Spellweaver:

To begin, I would like to thank my family and teachers for supporting me and urging me to become a better writer, and all of my friends who are there for me and I am there for them. Most importantly I give thanks to Judith Kristen for coming to our school and giving me the chance to publish my poems.

From Diana Casas:

I want to thank my siblings for understanding me and loving me. As well, I want to thank my mother who helped me to live throughout this difficult life. Also, I want to thank my ESL teacher, Mrs. Mose, who helped me to learn the English language. Finally, I want to thank Mrs. Rojas, who was there for me when I didn't speak this language at all. Thanks to everyone who helped me to be who I am now. I love you all.

From Francisco Colon:

I would like to say thank you to my school for giving me this great opportunity to be an author and especially to Judith Kristen for her kindness and patience throughout this project. I also want to thank my Mom, my sister, Christina, and last but not least, I want to thank God for my many blessings.

From Makepeace Cotto:

I want to say thanks to my mother, Kathy Soto, and to my step dad, Onil, for supporting me in everything I do. To my best friend/cousin/sister, Joanna Rivera, I love you girl, with all my heart. To: Erica, Marlyn, Sabrina, Pre, Fanni, Deanna, Yolanda, Stephany, Linda, Maria, Desire, Tiny, Trishy, Kenya, Kayla, Kia, Cristi, Jay-Jay, Sito, Alberto, Jonathan, Will, Qamar, Sam, PJ, TJ, Carlos, Tyree, Quince, Woo, Aaron, and everybody who always pushed me to the limit. I love you all. For those I forgot to mention, you know I love you and I'll be here for you all through thick and thin.

From Lisa Curcio:

I would like to thank my mother for helping me every step of the way and for being so supportive of what I do in life. Also, thanks to my "Ex" for giving me enough grief and angst to allow me to move on and yet inspire my work. Last but not least, my "Crush", who inspires me in the right way. And, to my friends and extended family, I love you all!

From Rob DiClementi:

Thanks to my parents for always being so supportive of everything I've done. Thanks also to my friends for having such a good influence on me, and ultimately, thanks to God for giving me the gift of life.

From Gregory Forest:

Thanks to my Mom, Dad, Aunt Gwen, Uncle Tyrone, Uncle Bernard, Mr. Abrams, Mr. Wisely and Lindenwold High School, and Superintendent Geraldine Carroll, for this splendid opportunity. Thanks to Mrs. Kristen for all of her help, structure, and guidance as well.

From: Desiree' Forrest:

I thank God for blessing me with the gift of writing. Thank you to Mr. Ranelli and Mrs. Kristen for the chance to display my work. Special Thanks to my best friends/sample readers, Makeda Smalls and Ebony Wesley, for the positive feedback. I love you both! Mr. Roddy and Ms. Ryan, thanks for teaching me to think outside of the box. Thanks to my mom Joyce, my brother, Jay, and my boyfriend. Thanks for everything; words can't express how much I love you all!

From Tyree Frierson:
I want to say thank you to Ms. Kristen and also say thank you to Lindenwold High School and Superintendent Geraldine Carroll, for giving me the opportunity to express myself. Much love and thanks to my mother and my grandmother, for always being there for me, and for keeping me out of trouble.

From Bonvincent Hernandez:
I'd like to thank the Lord for giving me all the strength and potential I possess. To my loving parents, Laura and Bonifacio, for raising me well, and for always being there for me. Lastly, I'd like to thank all of my friends, for I wouldn't be who I am today without them.

From Megan Herrera:
I would like to thank all of my teachers from grade one to grade ten. Each one of you has made a huge impact on my life. I would also like to thank Judith Kristen for this opportunity, and also I would like to thank my family and friends, for they are my inspiration.

From Jessica Kealey:
I would like to thank my Mom, Dad, sister, Jaclyn, best friends: Miranda, Mikey, Madalyn, Amy, and all of my friends and family. I also owe a lot to my teachers, especially the wonderful Mrs. Bubb, Mme. Raffner, Mrs. Dean, and Mrs. Zelis -- I couldn't have made it this far without you!

From Anna Kriner:
In loving memory of Kathleen Charlotte Kriner:
A life lost, an angel gained.

From Melinda Lee:

Much love and thanks to my Mom and cousin, Penny, for being so supportive of me as a person, as well as for supporting my work. A big thank you to my school, Lindenwold, for allowing this book to come into being. And a really big thank you to Judith Kristen for helping us realize our potential. I would like to thank my teachers for being honest with me about my stories and poems. I would like to say thank you to my family for encouraging me to do what I do best, be myself. If it weren't for them I really don't know if I could do my best. And again, to Judith Kristen, the one person that helped me with my grammar and spelling. So, thanks to all of you for helping me in my journey in becoming a writer and poet. Thank you for helping my voice to be heard.

From Michael Lipshultz:

I would like to thank my entire family: Mom, Dad, Jamie and Johnny, for always being there for me. Also I wish to thank Lindenwold High School for allowing Ms. Kristen to start the Teen Writers Guild, and also I would like to say thank you to all of my friends for inspiring me.

From David N. Megginson:

To my father, who taught me how to be a man. To my mother, who showed me what love really is. And to my brother, who makes sure that no matter what may come, there's always someone who makes life worth living.

From Antione McGee:

I would like to thank Judith Kristen for coming to my school and giving all of us this wonderful opportunity. I also want to thank my Aunt and my Grandmother for always loving me and supporting me. Also, thanks to: Bishop David G. Evan, Pastor Nicholas Smith, and Rev. Walker for giving me strength and encouragement through the hard times. Last but not least, I would like to thank God and my mother, Timicka McGee.

From Sarafina Muhammad:

I would like to thank my mother for always being there, my son for always putting a smile on my face, a thank you to God for seeing me through so much, and also to my teachers and friends at LHS. A special thank you to Judith Kristen for all of her help. I am very grateful.

From Caitlin Mullaney:

I **need** to thank the most important influences in my life: Ciarra, you have always been there for me. If it wasn't for you, I probably wouldn't even be here. For Taira: You were the first friend I had when I moved to New Jersey. You helped me make other friends and you were always so honest and kind. And to Sara: Out of ALL of my relatives you are one of the few people I truly look up to. Again, thank you all. I love you and never want to lose any of you. I would be lost without you in my life.

From Madalyn Natividad:

The people I would like to thank the most are not only my mother and closest friends, but also my friends' parents who have inspired me by showing me people *do* care and will help you and hold their arms out to you when you least expect it.

From Bhagyesh Nayi:

First of all, I wish to thank my family for teaching me good, strong family values. Those guidelines have made me the person I am today. And last, but not least, to all of my friends for being there with me through everything and always giving me support and encouragement.

From Victor Palillero:

First of all I want to thank God and all the persons who helped me change my life. I want to thank my mother and tell her I'm so sorry for everything I did wrong. I also want to thank all the people that are now helping me to make the right choices in my life. I want to say thank you to my second mom, my friend, and my best teacher, Miss Deborah Mosely-Duffy. She is a wonderful person who helped me in school and in my personal life. Last, but not least, I want to thank Miss Judith Kristen for giving me the opportunity that express my feelings, my anger, my joy, and for giving me respect in this space.

From Danielle Palombo:
I would like to give thanks to my friends who give me a lot of my inspiration and with whom I can be myself. Also, Thanks to my English teacher, Mrs. Bubb, who helped me become a better writer. I would like to give special thanks to my Mom and Dad for always encouraging me to be the best I can be. Finally, I would like to thank my great grandmother, Babci, for showing me the importance of family and being together.

From Ivan Alejandro Pineiro:
I would like to dedicate my part of the book to my grandmother, who recently passed away. I would like to thank my Mom, Dad, and sister for helping me when I needed it the most, and for inspiring me. I would like to also thank my friends and other family members, and my teachers, for their support all throughout my life. I also want to say thank you to GOD, because with him, all things are possible.

From Cynthia Recarte:
I want to dedicate this book to my parents and also to my school. I want to thank my teachers, Mrs. Mosly Duffy and Mrs. Rojas-Driscoll, the ones who have helped me so much here in this country. They are the ones who helped me when I didn't know how to write and speak English. Also, I want to thank Lindenwold High School for bringing me this opportunity to write in this book as well as to study and learn about so many things in this wonderful school. Thanks, as well, to God and my parents for all the opportunities they have given to me throughout my life.

From Brittany Robertson:
First of all, I want to thank Jesus Christ. Now, for my earthly people: Thanks to Mom, my constant, and to my sisters, love y'all! To my Aunts: Hazel, Chrissy, and Katherine for being there when Mom wasn't, and to my Uncle Andre and Latonya, I love ya with all my heart. Also, to my Dad, David, and my four best friends: Aliccia, Mario, Abby, and Brionna. A special thanks to Mrs. Kristen and her husband, Andrew, for your time and talent to give all of us this wonderful opportunity.

From Symone Robinson:
First of all I would like to thank my mother for frustrating me every day and for giving me a place to escape and find inspiration. I would also like to thank my support system which consists of: Amara Bowen, Dana Terry, Tiffany Einsinger, Lisa Curcio, and last, but not least – Mrs. Bubb, the best teacher on earth!

From: Makeda Robinson-Smalls
I would like to thank my mother for always inspiring me to write and motivating me my entire life. I would also like to thank Desiree Forrest, Brittany Smith and Shakierah Cannady for always believing in me, even when I did not believe in myself. Lastly, I would like to thank Mr. Roddy and Ms. Ryan for helping me develop my talent and share it with the world.

From Yeni Rodriguez:
I dedicate my writings to God, family, friends, and my ESL teacher. To them, I give thanks for always being there for me.

From Ariana Ross:
Thanks to my Father, no matter what idiotic things I may do in my life I know you'll always be there for me. To my Mom, I know we have our differences, but you love me, and I love you, too. To Ian, if you were not here, I don't know where I

would be right now. To Mom-mom and Pop-pop, you help my family more times than I can count, and you're still doing it, thank you for being there, I love you. To Grandma, you are such a beautiful person and you accept me for who I am, I love you. To all of my aunts, uncles, cousins, and friends, all of you have touched my heart and I thank you.

From Karla Siete:
First of all, I want to thank GOD for all the obstacles he has pulled me through. I have learned many things from all of these obstacles. I also want to thank Mrs. Mosely-Duffy for supporting me; not just as a student, but also like a daughter. She is like a second mother to me in school. She is a wonderful person who helps me in school and in life.

From Tashae Smith:
I would like to thank God, first and foremost, for putting me on this earth to write this story. Also thanks to my mom and dad for giving me life. Thanks as well to my English teachers: Mr. Rosetti, Mr. Abrams, and Mrs. Borst for teaching me how to write. And, last but not least, to Mike for giving me a story to write.

From Dana Terry:
I would like to thank my parents, for creating new ways for me to express myself. Without my father, I would have NEVER learned to play bass guitar, or sing...he has always been my world, and I love him so much! To my mother: for always lending a hand to the needy. Her goodness inspires me! Also HUGE thanks to my BEST friends: Becky, Amara, Jessica, Symone and Frankie. I would also like to thank God... for everything he has ever done for me! I would also like to thank Green Day, and H.I.M. for showing me that being an "outcast" isn't all that bad. And, thanks Aunt Linda, for being my "other" mother, and for always loving me. To my grandparents, who used to baby-sit me and take good care of me from the time I was two until I was seven! They mean the world to me! AND, finally, to my brother, Justin: I

always seem to HATE him, as most sisters hate their brother. But I love Justin and I always know that if something happens to me he would be the first one there to catch me.

From Abrianna Wilp-O'Neill

I want to thank my mom for always being there for me. She has helped me through so much and I do not think that I could have gotten this far without her. I want to thank my Pop-Pop, and my grandma, also my little sister. To the best friends that I could ever have: You always have my back and I will always have yours. Thanks to my high school teachers and thank you so much, Ms. Kristen, for making this possible for us!

From Briana Woodruff:

I would like to thank God for blessing me with my talent. I would also like to thank Lindenwold and Ms. Kristen for this once in a lifetime opportunity. Love and Thanks as well to my family: my mother, grandmother, and especially to my dear grandfather, George Gibbs, who looks down upon me from heaven.

I love you all.

The test of the morality of a society
is what it does for its children.
- Deitrich Bonhoeffer

Lindenwold High School
Home of the Lions

~ Lindenwold High School ~

Lindenwold High School opened its doors on September 10, 2001 welcoming students from throughout the local community. The mission of the Lindenwold High School has been to develop lifelong learners who are ready to conquer the challenges of college or the workplace by having the skills to react to real-life unpredictable situations.

Our small school environment allows teachers and students to build bonding relationships. Our educational beliefs center around the trust and respect needed to foster true learning experiences. Students at Lindenwold are provided with an educational experience that prepares them for challenges that lie ahead. On top of all of our academic values Lindenwold High School places great emphasis on character education and development.

The Lindenwold experience includes a full array of sports teams and extra-curricular activities throughout the school year. Our staff and students produced a variety of plays and concerts that entertain the entire Lindenwold community. The high school also sponsors many other clubs that serve the community such as the Interact Club, LEO Club, and Student Government Services. And now, to add to this most prestigious list:

The Teen Writers Guild of Lindenwold High School.

On top of these amenities the staff fosters a caring atmosphere that illustrates pride in their profession and a deep feeling of ownership in the school. The students bring life to the environment through honesty, caring, and pride. Together we succeed in producing positive citizens for our society - for generation after generation to come.

FOREWORD

It is with great pleasure that I introduce you, dear reader, to this wonderful book,
"Hear Us ROAR!" – a record of the creativity and ingenuity of forty-one young people who are students at Lindenwold High School in Lindenwold, New Jersey. These writings are the product of a great deal of effort on the parts of many caring people.

A couple of years ago, I met Judith Kristen, a local author of teen literature and other writings. Judith has a zest and energy very few of us have. In addition, she loves young people and they know it. Above all, she has a strong belief in the innate capabilities of young people. I was moved by her work with teens at Frankford High School in Philadelphia and introduced her to educational leaders in Camden County, New Jersey. Several of them were also moved by her convictions; and one of them, Ms. Geraldine Carroll, Superintendent at the Lindenwold School District, had the vision to invite Judith to Lindenwold High School to repeat her Frankford High School project at Lindenwold. Mr. Frank Ranelli, the principal at Lindenwold High School shares the creative vision and has been supportive and encouraging throughout the recruiting, writing and editing process which has led to the production of this amazing book.

For many of these young emergent writers, putting this book together was a Herculean task which took sweat, persistence, and courage. I am honored to have been a small part of this marvelous undertaking.

I guarantee you will read with tears in your eyes and a song in your heart.

Genevieve Lumia
Education Specialist
Camden County Office of Education
November, 2006

From our Principal –
Mr. Frank Ranelli

The formation of the Lindenwold High School
Teen Writers Guild has allowed our student writers the ability to have their voices heard. Our
talented young writers have taken every opportunity to allow their readers to realize their matu-
rity and vast experiences, as well as their passion
for the written word. I am honored to be a part
of the project and truly proud of the work these

students have accomplished. My hope is that this book project will inspire young people to realize the various avenues to communicate their emotions. I would like to thank our resident author, Judith Kristen, for her vision and enthusiasm during the creation of this book. I would also like to express sincere gratitude to our Superintendent, Geraldine Carroll, our Board of Education, and our wonderful staff for the constant support given to our students during this wonderful opportunity.

You can teach a student a lesson for a day;
But if you can teach him to learn by
creating curiosity,
he will continue the learning process
for as long as he lives.

- Clay Bedford

~From our Lindenwold School District Superintendent ~ Ms. Geraldine Carroll

Students spend their entire educational career reading literature, learning about writers, and wondering why they need to spend so much time picking apart stories and poems written by a bunch of "Old dead guys". These teens also are the most often misunderstood and least often accepted members of their community. **Hear Us ROAR!** finally gives them a voice and gives relevancy to all that they have learned. Watching them work, struggle, laugh and cry as they express their fears, dreams, and aspirations has been even more rewarding than seeing the final product, a published book.

Congratulations to the warm and talented writers who were willing to take a risk to lay open for peer and public examination, their deepest thoughts and feelings and for working so hard to make sure that their poems and stories would touch the reader as literature is meant to do. I would also like to thank Judith Kristen for her energy, enthusiasm, and guidance, and Leslie Woodward, Frank Ranelli, and the teachers at Lindenwold High School for their support of this project, as well as to acknowledge Genevieve Lumia for bringing Judith to us. It is this kind of commitment that brings out the best in our kids and turns them from students into authors and poets.

Geraldine Carroll
November, 2006

HEAR US ROAR!

By

The Teen Writers Guild of
Lindenwold High School

It requires wisdom to
understand wisdom:
the music is nothing if the
audience is deaf.

- Walter Lipmann

The Written Works of
Makeda Robinson-Smalls

WISDOM

Where does my path lead
What turns must I take
What happens when I encounter
A fork in the road
And don't know
Which way to go
What happens
When I take a detour
And end up far from my path
What happens when I get lost
And no one is able to show me the way back home
What happens when I'm all alone
And fall into temptation
What happens when I waste my time
Still never finding my way
What happens when my time has passed
And I have lived my last dreadful day
It is then that I will understand
The reality of this world and its beauty
But then it's too late
For me to appreciate
Because my life has slipped away
Hasn't it?
We are all a result of what we have thought.
So…
Think what could happen
If you'd rethink now.

Even Still

You used to say you loved me
But now I know that was a lie
I gave you my heart
You threw it back full force
I gave you my soul
You ripped it in two, but of course, I still hadn't
learned
With you I never do
I've tried my best to close my heart
But that doesn't stop me from loving you
You're the best and the worst thing that ever
happened to me
You gave me the chance to love
But with that chance
Came a price
This I did not know
And when you threw my love away
You killed me and my chance to grow
But even still
No matter what I do
I cannot seem to stop myself from feeling the way I
feel for you
It seems as though
I am destined to spend my whole life
Loving you

Apathy is the glove into
which evil slips its hand.

- Bodie Thoene

Makeda Robinson-Smalls was born December 27, 1989. She has been writing poetry for about six years. Makeda has completed two books of poetry and is in the process of writing a young adult novel. She hopes to become a well-known poet in years to come.

So, save a place on your bookshelf for Makeda's poetry!

Try any damn thing you like, no matter how boringly normal or outrageous. If it works, fine. If it doesn't, toss it. Toss it even if you love it.

- Stephen King

The Written Works of
Amara Bowen

Spica

You, often eclipsed by the moon
Luna the one that you really despise
Out of daylight's darkening cocoon
The star of midnight will slowly arise

Defeating the darkness
with lustrous haze
Incandescent and full of life
I'm dazzled, mesmerized,
and under daze
And with your fate you are at strife

Bitter elegies of perpetuity
You're the Virgo's ear of wheat
No sense of eschatology
Nor death will you meet
No violent emission
Just honest endeavor
And without the god's permission
Spica will reign forever

The Night That Mercury Cried

We lay along the ecliptic line
And watch our sunset die
Caress the mane of Neptune
And listen to Mercury cry.

I'm down here standing on the sidewalk
My heart is up there with you
I only whisper for you my love
I only whisper for you.

Only this night is the sky so bright
The stars are silvers pride
This is the night I realized I love you
The night that Mercury cried.

The man with insight enough to admit his limitations comes nearest to perfection.

- Johann Wolfgang von Goethe

Amara Bowen is a sixteen year-old sophomore at Lindenwold High School. Her interests are: reading, writing, music, microbiology, drawing, and astronomy. Her favorite classes are English and Science. In the future Amara hopes to attend Berklee School of Music. She has four brothers and four sisters.

All that we are is the result of
what we have thought.
The mind is everything.
What we think, we become.

- Buddha

The Written Works of
David N. Megginson

A Biography of Me

My life has not been perfect, neither has it been the complete chaos of others my age. I cannot recount the horrible abuse from a loved one, cannot tell of the sleepless nights and the endless tears, as some of my peers can. Mine is not an obvious pain, but it hurts all the same. My brother Johnathan and I have coped with all that has been handed to us, and although we have not had the worst possible lives, ours is a sad experience nonetheless. I do not write this in search of someone to sympathize with me. That would be foolish. I write this to remind myself that there are others who need me to care and pay attention as much as I wish people would.

My parents were good people. My father was a minister who spent much of his time visiting and caring for people's souls, and he was loved in the community for his desire to help others. My mother cared for my brother and I at home, and also helped at the church. They loved each other very much. Sadly, they were in a large amount of debt due to mistakes in their youth. Together, they lived a difficult life for many years, often making hard choices that might permanently affect their children's futures. In the midst of these times, our mother and father made every effort to ensure a happy and loving home. John and I were home schooled, and in spite of our hardships, my father worked most of the day and a paper route at night to make sure our mother could stay home and teach us.

In May of 2000, our father died quite unexpectedly and tragically at the age of 37 by being crushed underneath a car. On his night paper route, he was very tired and fell asleep at the wheel. He veered off the road and crashed into an embankment on the side, damaging his car. Being close to our grandparent's home, my dad borrowed my grandfather's car to finish the paper route. Because of my father's exhaustion though, he again fell asleep while driving only to crash into a second embankment, breaking an axle on the car. When my grandfather's car was towed to our house, my father was trying to repair the damage to it when the screw jack bracing the vehicle collapsed, bringing it down on him. My father's daytime business associate found him moments later, but it was too late. The paramedics said that my father probably died instantly, as the car had hit his head and throat.

My mother was heartbroken. He was the only man she had ever loved, and to not have him anymore was beyond her ability to cope with. She receded into her own world, and while she was still "functional" by society's standards, she was never the same. My brother and I learned to clean, cook, and coexist in her stead, knowing that we should do these things for her, and allow her to mourn in her own time. One morning after church, my mother, my brother, and I were exiting onto a highway from the church's side road when the brakes in the car gave out. The shop that had replaced the brakes had failed to properly repair the automobile. We careened into the road, just as another vehicle was passing.

They topped the hill to fast to stop. Our car was struck on the driver's side in the front, and we skidded across the freeway into the parking lot across the road. I was the first one awake, and I saw my brother and mother still unconscious. Although I did my best to rouse them, only my brother would ever open his eyes again. My mother died in February of 2002, less than two years after my father's death. Things became a blur as funereal arrangements were made and family members talked about "what would become of us". When all was said and done, we decided to stay with our aunt Carmen, favoring a relative in the same town we had lived in. John and I wanted to stay close to our friends in Virginia, and thought this the logical choice. Sadly, location was not the only factor we should have considered.

Unbeknownst to us, our aunt had a history of "help-ing" the less fortunate she encountered if they had anything to offer. The large amount of money that our parents had left behind for us was consumed on a daily basis, and we were constantly reminded that we did not have enough. She would *have* to take more from the savings if we were to live comfortably. During this time, John and I were subjected to Carmen's fanatical Christian beliefs. Over time, the naivety faded, and my brother and I slowly realized the horror we had now become part of. It is my own personal belief that our aunt is bipolar, although she refuses to accept that opin-ion and refuses to seek treatment. She has asked me in tears what is wrong with her, yet insists that God is the answer, and most of the time she says she does not have a problem.

Regardless of the real motives or problems behind her actions, John and I eventually realized that we were now between a rock and a hard place with my aunt. We began to seek an out, knowing that our parents had friends that would take us regardless of the situation. I personally escaped for a while to live with another minister, the man who had taken over the church my father had been in charge of. I saw all the clearer the chaos and irregularity of our lives, but eventually returned, not wishing my brother to suffer when I was free. Carmen had refused to let him go, saying that he had no wish to leave "his home".

We began to seek an escape, and tried in secret to con-tact others who might help us get free. She caught wind of our plans one day when she accidentally overheard a con-versation between John and one of our conspirators. She exploded then, but it seemed that the situation was forgotten afterward. A few weeks later I was taken out of school for a "doctor's appointment", but 8 hours later found myself here in New Jersey. I was turned over to my Uncle Robert, who had warned me long ago of my aunt's treachery, but I was either too foolish or too bent on staying in Virginia to listen then. He was still on my side, and offered to help me in any way I saw fit, giving me his advice but allowing me to make the decision. Although he thought I should return to my Uncle David in Virginia, he made his home open, and I decided to stay in New Jersey, far away from my Aunt Carmen's reach. Shortly thereafter, my Aunt consented to release my brother as well. We had finally run out of money, and were no use to her anymore.

Carmen has tried to contact us further over the years, asking for money and "apologizing" for what she did, saying that although we were wrong, she was willing to take us back and "work things out". John and I have learned the danger of her words. Although we now have little to live on, we are happy here. My Uncle Robert and my Aunt Sharon have helped us greatly. We are now getting prepared for college, myself this year and my brother next year. I am currently in the top twenty percent of my class, meaning that I qualify for the New Jersey STARS program. My brother has had constantly rising scores over the past years, and is currently doing his best to bring up his GPA.

I have never cried for my parents. I mean, I shed a few tears at the hospital when they informed me that my father had passed, but that was it. When they told John and I that our mother had died, we shared a look that said, "what will we do", but there were no tears to cry. People have told me that there is a danger in not crying, and to that affect, perhaps they are right. Although I don't see it now, people have warned me that some time in the future, the pain and anger might arise at a place and time I may not like. Maybe they are right. I think of it another way though. My parents would not have wanted me to sit and weep for hours for them. They were always a good and practical couple, and the voice of my father inside tells me that he would have wanted me to be sensitive, but at the same time, he would say not to cry over spilt milk.

I have no tragic ending. This is not the story of a young man that has fallen with no hope. This is simply the account of one person and the sadness of his life. The fall, long and hard, and the inevitable climb back toward a normal life.

I am not defeated. Quite the contrary, their life and death have made me everything I am, and it would be a waste to let their legacy pass with them.

I will carry on their story.

That tale...is not yet over.

Ethereal

The trees whisper their silent words to
me.
Listen to that.
The beauty, the splendor is absolute.
Perfection lies in her eyes.
Angels grace these woods today clothed
in light.
This is life's obsession.
Filter through, trickling in and out of
view.
We play the games we love.
The earth, the skies, purest grace.
Water runs swiftly, little feet splash
among the waves.
Dancing, weaving the dreams of
strangers.
We watch with closed eyes.

--David Megginson

Carpe Diem
(Seize the day)

- Horace

David N. Megginson is eighteen-years-old and in his senior year at Lindenwold High School. Although he loves writing, he plans to attend college and pursue a doctorate in mathematics. In his spare time, he enjoys working with computers and hanging out with his friends. He loves his brother, John, more than life itself.

❧

Everything changes when you change.

- Jim Rohn

The Written Works of
Caitlin Mullaney

Abused and **Unwanted**

Alone....

Forgotten....

Abused....

How did you let it get this way?
Did you *really* think it would go away?

The pain is so very real.
I just wish you could know how they feel.

Living in fear day to day,
Never really knowing what to say.

They hide the bruises under their clothes,
Making sure no one knows.

For scars, stories are told.
But don't these stories sound a bit too… ?

These children are dying! Don't you see?
Why won't you believe me?

Oh, it's because they're alive and they have no visible
marks you say?
Torture can go much deeper, OK?!!

You can be alive whilst being dead.
You heard what I said!

Words hurt just the same.

I've heard that…

Parents will be parents
and
Kids will be kids
but…
Isn't that just an excuse

So there's no one to blame?

NO WAY!!!

Listen closely for their song.
It may be loud.
It may be silent.
Either way
It's still strong.

The lyrics are left upon thousands of pillows cases.
From thousands of faces.
From thousands of races.

All want to belong.
All want to end their sad song.

Some end it themselves, unfortunately,

without anyone's help.
So, in the middle of the night, they…

Others end with a final blow from mom and dad.
You can't tell me that's not truly sad.

For most people, moms and dads are heroes.
But for far too many, they are horrific zeros.

Between drugs and booze, or whatever they choose
Parents think they have nothing to lose.

So destroying your own flesh and blood's life is okay???
What are these people thinking?!

The **pain** they cause, the pain **you** let happen
Kills far, far, too many innocent children.
Have a heart, use your mind, grow some character!
And stop this holocaust of our youth like **<u>REAL</u>** men
and women.

~Caitlin Mullaney

Even though you may want to move forward in your life, you may have one foot on the brakes. In order to be free, we must learn how to let go. Release the hurt. Release the fear. Refuse to entertain your old pain. The energy it takes to hang onto the past is holding you back from a new life. What is it you would let go of today?

- Mary Manin Morrissey

A positive attitude causes a chain reaction of positive thoughts, events, and outcomes. It is a catalyst, a spark that creates extraordinary results.

Caitlin Mullaney was born on December 25th, 1991. Ms. Mullaney is currently a freshman at Lindenwold High. She loves to watch movies, listening to music, hanging out with her friends, and surfing the net. Caitlin isn't sure what she wants to do after graduation, but she is exploring many options. One thing Caitlin IS sure of is that whatever she does, she will follow her heart doing it, and she will *always* be herself no matter what anyone says or thinks of her. She will always be her own "person."

Just because you're a perfectionist
doesn't mean you're perfect.

- Jack Nicholson
...describing Stanley Kubrick

The Written Works of
Dana Terry

Sacrifice

Everyday somebody loses a friend
To the dangers of this world
And
As we lose one another a new soul is brought
Every ending
Has a new beginning
But we can not forget
The ones that went away
For their souls will never die
Every time the sacrifice is made
another one cries
Hoping the world will never die
All we can do
Is pray
Every ending
Has a new beginning
But we can not forget
The ones that went away
For their souls will never die
The world is full of empty souls
Trying to find their place
Hoping they are not forgotten
With every single day
Every ending
Has a new beginning
But we can not forget
The ones that went away
For their souls will never die
For as we grow older
Others souls begin to fade
And then
The sacrifice is made

Always There

Even though the world is tough at times
You can always make it through
No matter where you go or what you do
I'll always be there for you

The world may be a difficult place
And you'll always need a friend
But in the end we are all the same

A friend is a friend is a friend

The tragedy of Modern Man is not
that he knows less and less about
the meaning of his own life but
that it bothers him less and less.

- Vaclav Havel

Dana Terry was born July 19, 1991. She is a multi-talented musician. Dana plays clarinet, bass guitar, and she sings! Ms. Terry is a big fan of alternative rock/punk music. Her hobbies consist of hanging with friends, playing in her band, playing sports, listening to music, and skateboarding. Dana comes from a divorced household; she has one brother, a step-brother, and step-sister. Her favorite colors are red and green. And, she is blessed to have five of the best friends in the whole world: Amara, Ariana, Becky, Jessica, and Frankie!

No matter how much I prove and prod,
I can not quite believe in God;
But oh, I hope to God that
He unswervingly
Believes in me.

Attributed to E. Y. Harburg

The Written Works of
Ariana Ross

Bliss

I'm told I look so pretty
Dressed all up in your clothes
I'm not only your doll
I am your puppet

You say you love me
As long as I dance to your tune
You pull my strings and I will
Dance, dance, dance

A painted on smile
So it would seem I'm never sad
Always grinning
As my feet move to the haunting melody

Painted hues
They never cry
Emotionless face
This is what you call beauty

You say you see all that I am
All that I can be
I wish I would rip out your eyes
To see what you see

Placed in front of a mirror
I wait for it to break
I can see all my cracks, my scratches
They cannot hide under your pretty clothes

You whisper nice things to me
The lies
That you call complements
Almost burn my ear

I don't speak up
Rejecting your words only bring more lies
So I listen
And keep quiet

Now you are done
And I am placed aside
Not controlled any longer
But I don't forget the strings

Painted eyes look into the now dark room
Am I lonely?
Am I sad?
Of course not...
Just look at my smile

Love can sometimes be magic. But magic can sometimes...just be an illusion

- Javan

This high school student, by the name of Ariana Ross, is one terrific ball of energy. Her likes are: anime, video games, chatting on AIM, and role-playing. She hopes to someday become a great Manga artist who is loved the world over.

Better keep yourself clean and bright;
you are the window through
which you must see the world.

- George Bernard Shaw

The Written Works of
Danielle Palombo

The Girl in the Mirror

I stood there with my eyes closed,
Listening
Waiting

I could hear my heart beat.

I prepared myself for what I would see.

I opened my eyes.

In the mirror in front of me, there was someone I did not
recognize.
Who **was** this person?

I detested the odd looking stranger.
She looked fake and unreal.

And she was.

I changed into my old outfit
I re-combed my hair.
I felt better.

As I left, I glanced in the mirror one last time.

I thought to myself,
This is a person I know,
This is who I am, who I really like.

And…

If people don't like me this way?

Well, just look at what they're missing!

Danielle Palombo is a sixteen-year-old Lindenwold High School student. She lives with her Mom, Dad, and little sister, Dana. Danielle has a great love for art as well as for writing. She has been drawing for as long as she can remember and is quite talented. Another big part of her life is Girl Scouts. She has been a member for eleven years! Ms. Palumbo is grateful to be blessed with so many wonderful people in her life.

Character cannot be developed
in ease and quiet. Only through
experience of trial and suffering can
the soul be strengthened, ambition
inspired, and success achieved.

- Helen Keller

The Written Works of
Vanessa Brown

Momma's Words

Growing up wit momma,
She ain't doing so well,
No job and no money,
But through those obstacles
She's my very own motivational speaker.
Gives me life lessons,
That I take and reserve in my heart,

But then I'm like,
Why should I listen to you,
You not making it in life,
You messed up,
And now you want to reprimand me?
I can't understand.
You don't help yourself,
And now you wanna help me?
Why you think you got all the answers?
Telling me that one thing goes in one ear and
out the other,
Are you not hearing me,
I TOLD you I listen.
Over and over you tell me to never give up.
and never lose faith
Take pride in everything I do,
Cause momma ain't raise no stupid little girl,
You told me to do better than you,
Cause I can do anything I put my mind to.
Don't mean to be rude,
But momma got a lot of attitude,
When I tell her,
I'm doin' what I wanna do,
Even though I don't know what I wanna do.

My mind tells me one thing,
My heart tells me another,
Dang, momma…
Why you ain't tell me you wasn't gonna be here?
Don't you know that these are the hardest and most
complex times of my life?!
I listened to you,
I did
But where are you now?
I have so much to deal with.
I need to confide in you,
I need your love,
and your words, your words,
I **need** my momma's words.

The test of literature is, I suppose,
whether we ourselves live more intensely
for the reading of it.

- Elizabeth Drew

Vanessa Capri Brown is a seventeen-year-old junior at Lindenwold High School. When Vanessa's not playing tennis in the fall or basketball in the winter, you can find her writing in her diary or listening to music. She has a very outgoing and sweet personality that shines through because of her positive attitude toward life. Vanessa loves being with her family and friends, because they mean the world to her. She lives with her father and stepmother and visits her mother in Indianapolis every summer. Ms. Brown continues to be a role model for her four siblings by getting good grades and staying out of trouble! Vanessa is a very inspirational writer and she always strives to be the best she can be.

Great spirits have always
encountered violent opposition
from mediocre minds.

- Albert Einstein

The Written Works of
Lisa Curcio

Free

Feeling free
Living life to the fullest
Making the most of who I am
That's what I need to do
To have a better life
To get away from what's stopping me
Getting away

Escape now

Valentine's Day

Love **is for** Valentine's Day
When you are alone
You hope
You wish
You pray
To find the one who likes
you
If indeed someone does
A secret crush
An anonymous love letter
What can you do
To find out
Who likes the real you???

Remember, people will judge you
by your actions, not your intentions.
You may have a heart of gold - but
so does a hard-boiled egg.

- Anon.

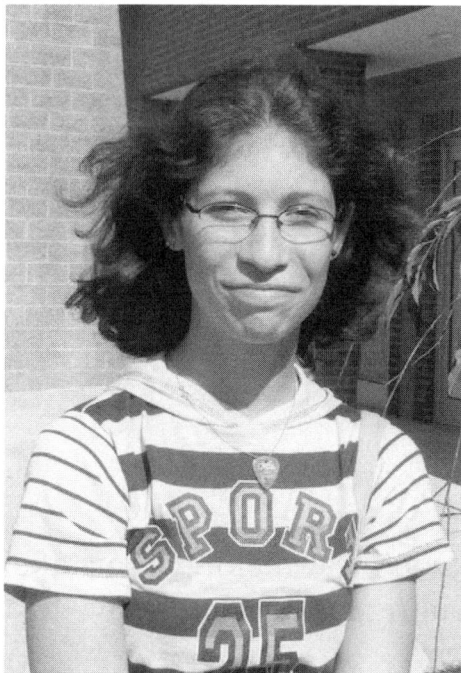

Lisa Curcio is a sixteen-year-old artist who enjoys reading, writing, poetry, painting, and sketching. Upon graduation, she wants to live in California, and hopefully she will attend Berkeley, do well, and just have a good and happy life in general! If anyone can do it, Lisa… you can!

Don't fear making a mistake;
fear failing to learn and move forward.

- Pilip Humbert

The Written Works of
Mike Lipshultz

Live Like There's No Tomorrow

As I lay there very still...I hear nothing

Nothing.

I wonder if I'll ever make it home.

Will I make it home to fight...to fight the good fight?

Will I make it home to see that glorious sight?

I wonder where *she* thinks I am.

I wonder if she's looking for me.

Will she ever *find* me?

Wait!

I see a light.

Am I *dead*?

"Here's my shoulder child, rest your head."

"Is *this*... heaven?"

"Are *you*... Jesus?"

"You're not ready child. You have a great life ahead.

Go back to her.

Wake up...wake up from this sleep … it's not your time.

Live life as you should. Live life like there is no
tomorrow."

I should.

I will.

I AM!

Michael is a hard-working student at Lindenwold High School. He particularly likes listening to music and enjoys Theatre Arts tremendously. Mike is relatively new to the world of writing, but he got the hang of it quickly. His work, "Live Like There's No Tomorrow", is an excellent example of what he can do. We hope to read more of Michael's work in the near future!

The world is not respectable; it is mortal,
tormented, confused, deluded forever;
but it is shot through with beauty, with
love, with glints of courage and laughter;
and in these, the spirit blooms timidly,
and struggles to the light amid the thorns.

- George Santayana

The Written Works of
Briana Woodruff

OVERCOME!

A woman once told me that life is a mountain to be climbed
and we should do our best to get to the very top.
Every time I have a _low_ point in my life, I move down that
mountain as if it were a landslide.
But, somehow, I never quite touch rock bottom, and again, I
struggle to rise.

But then I see you.

A sight for sore eyes.

All of a sudden time seems to stand still.

And I can feel

We are one.

As if I'm within you somehow.

Complete.

Solid.

With you I'm dying to live to the fullest.
Without you I was living to die.
I will forever think of you as my guardian angel.
A beautiful spirit that fell to me from the heavens above**.**
I reach the mountain top with you and because of you.

I triumph.
I overcome!

Briana Woodruff is just fourteen years old, and yet she is quite an accomplished writer. Her hobbies are (of course) writing, as well as singing and drawing. Briana has three brothers: Marvin, Lamar, and Ashawn, and one sister, Tameka. Ms. Woodruff hopes to attend Julliard upon graduation so that she can pursue a career in vocal arts. We will be hearing much more from the talented Miss Woodruff in the future!

But now abide faith, hope,
love, these three;
but the greatest of these is love.

- First Corinthians, Chapter 13

The Written Works of
Francisco Colon

"Faith"

*The Everlasting power I constantly feel in my
heart, tells me of dangers within the mighty
universe.*

*But, as a person, a brother, a son, an uncle, a
cousin, a grandson, and most importantly, a
friend forever, I rise to meet that challenge with
my double-sided blade in the ready position!*

*I run breathing heavily toward what ails me,
lifting that righteous blade above my head,
letting it fill with affirmation and holy love.*

I swing!

And I swing with all my might, lopping its head off.

Looking though the evil

*Seeing the secret desires I could have sewn, the
dangers I could cause within the war zone which
I could have called my soul.*

*I looked behind me as I held the omniscient sword
on my shoulder and I looked upon that damnable
spirit which has caused me so much grief, and I see
the horror I could have caused within my personal
universe and I reflect upon that.*

*At that exact moment I looked up into the
starry skies, up toward the heavens,*

I knew what I had to do.

*I folded my hands together and then I began the
most powerful act in the known universe - Prayer.*

*I prayed to my savior asking his help, hopeful
that he might hear my desperate voice for his
guidance and holy love.*

*My Incredible faith in my Lord Jesus Shall
Never, Ever Falter.*

Francisco Colon is a senior at Lindenwold High School. He is eighteen years old and lives happily at home with his mother, Luz who is extremely supportive of her son. Francisco's hobbies are: reading, drawing, and playing video games. Upon graduation he hopes to attend either Collins College Tech School or The Philadelphia Art Institute.

Whatever Francisco chooses to do in life, for certain he will succeed!

If you think you're beaten, you are;
If you think you dare not, you don't;
If you'd like to win, but think you can't,
It's almost a cinch you won't.
If you think you will lose, you're lost;
For out in the world we find,
Success begins with a fellow's will,
It's all in the state of mind.

If you think you're outclassed, you are;
You've got to think high to rise.
You've got to hustle before
You can ever win a prize.
Life's battles don't always go
To the stronger or faster man,
But sooner or later the man who wins
Is the one who thinks he can.

- Walter D. Wintle,

The Written Works of
Tyree Frierson

But I'm Alive!

I'm from the hood
Where the tears never end
In the game on call
---Round like a ball
Yeah it's lookin' sunny
But the rain's gonna fall

Roamin' through these mean streets, I be on guard
'Cause niggazs stealin' lives
Faster'n stealin' cars
But me, I'm still alive
'Cause I'm climbin' up these bars
Yeah, *I'm* still alive 'cause I'm climbin' up these bars

Then I stop to look around
And my homies' all gone
I'm the last of the last
And I'm holdin' on strong

Some say that I ain't earned it
So break it down and burn it
But I'm rebuilding life
'Cause I'm real
And I'm determined
Yeah.
I'm real
I'm determined
I'm alive.
Yeah.
I'm real
I'm determined
I'm alive.

Tyree Frierson is a sixteen-year-old sophomore at Lindenwold High School. He is new to the world of short stories and poetry, but he enjoyed expressing himself through the work that you have just read.

Tyree's dream is to live in Atlanta, Georgia, and become a cornerback for the Atlanta Falcons. Is there a Super Bowl ring in his future? Let's hope so!

Write quickly and you will
never write well.
Write well, and you will
soon write quickly.

- Marcus Fabius Quintilianus, 65 A.D.

The Written Works of
Melinda Lee

Boredom

Sitting here
… bored _all_ day
People asking if I'm okay
Staring out far into space
Wish these people would

GET
OUTTA
MY
FACE!!!

Anger

Anger shows its ugly face
But why in school,
Well, it's commonplace
With tests and work and things to do
I'd be angry... wouldn't you?

Courage is not the towering oak
that sees storms come and go;
it is the fragile blossom that
opens in the snow.

- Alice Mackenzie Swaim

Melinda Lee is nineteen years old and has a genuine love for art as well as the written word. Her own personal style, in terms of art and writing, is unique and makes you think twice.

Ms. Lee hopes to become an illustrator one day - adding artwork to her writing, creating a series of books all on her own. THAT would be her dream come true!

Melinda has the heart and passion to make it happen – stay tuned and watch for her star to shine!

A mother is the truest friend we have, when trials, heavy and sudden, fall upon us; when adversity takes the place of prosperity; when friends who rejoice with us in our sunshine, desert us when troubles thicken around us, still will she cling to us, and endeavor by her kind precepts and counsels to dissipate the clouds of darkness, and cause peace to return to our hearts.

- Washington Irving

The Written Works of
Antione McGee

The Love of My Life

Everyday I wake up thinking about her.
I wonder if I'll have just one more day with her.
Ever since my life began she was there.
She was there when first I opened my eyes, when I first walked, and when I said my first word.

Mom!

It didn't matter what it was, she was there.
There was never a second, minute, or hour of any day that she wasn't with me.
She and I are one, like the **Father and the Son**.
Our bond is strong.
Let me tell you why.
Our relationship can never be broken because when I was in her womb, we took of each other's hearts. So now it is my destiny to walk in her love and she in mine.
We all know that relationships have their ups and downs.
Let me give you an example:
You have fights, problems, disagreements, jealousy issues, and insecurities. With our relationship there aren't any fights because **Mom** will win all the time. We do have disagreements when I do something wrong, but when I admit my mistakes and ask for forgiveness, we're cool. The jealousy issues are not between her and me, but between my friends and cousins. They don't understand the bond I share with my mother and they are envious.
In my life, my mother plays the roles of both mother and father.
She does the best she can and whatever she can't handle she passes to my uncles, minister, or positive male role models in my life. When I was younger, I felt like I was an illegiti-

mate child because my father was not involved in my life. It is hard for a kid to understand why a parent who is supposed to love and support you is not there. My father would call or see me a few times a year. The pain I felt was indescribable and I would act out to cover up my pain. Then one day **God** helped me believe that I have all that I needed. He equipped my mother to give me everything I needed to succeed. I need to stop and give **God** praise for that right now. Really, I am blessed! I am in high school now and I know that if it weren't for my mother pushing me and demanding excellence, I wouldn't be here. I have forgiven my father and love him very much. I know one day he will recognize me as the gift that **God** blessed him with.

I believe that the first gift **God** blessed _me_ with is my mother. I believe **God** saw my mom, and said, "Into thine hands my servant shall be." The **Lord** said, "Together we will make him fishers of men for my glory!" My mother taught me discipline, respect, manners, and gave me all the educational tools that I needed to achieve in this world.

Mom, I want to let you know that I acknowledge and appreciate who you are and what you have done for me. I truly thank you! My life would not be complete without you. You truly possess all of the characteristics of what a mother should be. Your endless sacrifices, long working nights, and those special talks that we share, you are my friend!

Lord, I thank you for blessing me with a phenomenal mother.

I love you **Mom**! **Thank You**!

Dedicated to the love of my life,
Ms. Timicka McGee -- **my Mother**

All that I am, or hope to be, I
owe to my angel mother.

- Abraham Lincoln

Antione is a very ambitious young man. He hopes to become one of the world's youngest music and movie producers. Another passion of his is to attend Princeton University to study Criminal Law. In his mid-thirties, Antione hopes to become a preacher so that he can spread the good word, and help people who are lost, alone, and in need. We wish him much success in all of his positive endeavors!

How do I know what I think
until I see what I say?

- E. M. Forster

The Written Works of
Lessy Bonilla

Powerful,
practical paper
The walls of my education
The roof of my thoughts
The door to my soul
The window to my future

There once was a dirty cat "Hooks"
Giving the other cats bad looks
No one knows how he died
Not one single cat cried
He's with the other bad cat crooks

Beauty is being in harmony
with what you are.

- Peter Nivio Zarlenoa

Lessy Bonilla was born in Honduras. She is seventeen years old and in her earlier years she had quite a bit of sorrow. She is kind and gentle to others because she knows what suffering means. Lessy loves her family and she enjoys spending time with them. Miss Bonilla also spends much time involved with her church where at times she gives classes to younger children. Lessy loves to read interesting books that are full of the twists and turns of youth and the problems than come with them. Lessy Bonilla embraces the world, and the world embraces her. She is a star in her own right!

Our lives are not determined by what happens to us but by how we react to what happens, not by what life brings to us, but by the attitude we bring to life. A positive attitude causes a chain reaction of positive thoughts, events, and outcomes. It is a catalyst, a spark that creates extraordinary results.

- Anon

The Written Works of
Lisabeth Carl
Pen Name – Luna Spellweaver

The Fae

Into the woods we will roam,
Near the bushes and trees with gaps filling them,
In search for the magical faes that dwell within,
Laughing and singing like the child inside.

Tiny creatures all around,
Faes of every color that come to
play their little games.
It's like a wonderful dream seeing
them dance around,
Glistening like fresh snow falling to the ground.

Faes, Faes flying here and there,
Sparkling just like the sun's rays
in the month of May,
Spreading hope and joy to girls and boys.

As you enter the land of the fae,
The real world slowly falls away,
Leaving hate and crime behind,
In turn, it gives you peace of mind.

Now the day is done,
the lesson learned,
And here it is again…
Live each day in love and peace
As if it were your last,
Just the way that it was done
In dear sweet faeries past.

Alone

No one cares
that I feel alone in this world
I can't face these many fears
so I shed my tears
shielding myself from the outside world
while I sit alone
in my darkened room
No one cares
that I don't understand
They say that they're my friends
but betray me in the end
I can't take this torture anymore
and all this flight
No one cares
that I may seem invisible
They can't see the pain
that I hide inside
I conceal it with a smile
and a few good lies
Why can't anyone see
that this is simply me?
There really shouldn't be
much more to the fact
that I am here; yet not seen
Why am I alone?
Why does no one care
that I might not be there?
That I might not be anywhere...?
for too much longer!

Childhood

Oh so innocent
And not a care in the world
To be young again

- Luna SpellWeaver

L.M. Carl is a Senior at Lindenwold High School, but prefers to go by the magickal name, Luna SpellWeaver. She enjoys helping others with their problems, writing poetry, being a part of LHS's stage crew, and reading. Her family tree, as she says, is too messed up to explain in a brief bio, but she does acknowledge that she has five brothers and sisters. Upon graduation from Lindenwold, she hopes to attend college and become a psychologist and/or a photographer. We all wish her much success and happiness!

What doesn't kill you makes you stronger.

- Neitzche

The Written Works of
Victor Palillero

Life is Not a Game

My name is Victor Palillero.

I am seventeen years old and I come from a small town in Puebla, Mexico.

My life? Well, my life is more like a movie than a normal life.

When I was barely twelve years old, I started to hang out. The guys I was with showed me lots of things (more bad things than good things), and that's the way I learned to live life – BAD.

My own father never taught me the lessons a father should teach his son and so, I learned my "manly" life on the street.

When I was thirteen, I had a new group of friends and we did a lot of bad things, like spray paint the walls, set things on fire, shoot into the air with a real gun, etc. I didn't destroy property with paint. I painted murals about how I felt my life from the inside and outside. There were times that my friends used to go to another neighborhood and make trouble. Almost all of the time, we used to fight and sometimes we risked our lives. My brothers wanted to come with me, but I didn't want them to get into this mess. My mother suffered a lot for me. Sometimes she thought that I would never come back home. Sometimes my mother got desperate and she didn't know how stop me. She tried talking with me but her words entered in one of my ears and came out from the other one. She tried to ground me, too, but I used to escape. I remember one time that she was so mad at me she hit me with the broom really hard, hard enough that she broke it on my back. I got so mad that I ran away from home.

Soon I decided to hang in another neighborhood in another

town, and in that town we formed a gang. The name of our gang was L.G.N., The Latin Gangsters Nation.

The gang smoked, drank alcohol, they used to get high with drugs like marijuana, coco, and when they didn't have money, they huffed.

All the persons in my new town knew my name, and for all the wrong reasons. But in the street, in gangs, the badder and riskier things you did, the more popular you were, and at the time that was very important to me.

There once was a time that I was with four of my best friends. You could say that it was the first time that we were talking about how our lives would have grown in a different way. All of my friends were much too drugged, but I will always remember the words one of them told me., "If you have the opportunity to change your life, do it and don't let anybody stop you."

Did I listen? No. Not right away.

Soon, we were going to go to a party, so we got in the car, but for some strange reason me and my friend forgot our jackets, so we got out of the car to get them. Our friends didn't wait for us and they left to buy cigarettes. Me and my other friend waited for them for about ten minutes. We were about to leave when I saw my friend's car coming really fast in our direction. It was out of control! The car quickly turned over and crashed in to a light post so hard that the post fell onto the car. When I saw this happen I ran to the car to see if they were all okay. I looked at them in the car and their faces were all bloody. It was the hardest experience I ever had. When I saw them I couldn't even catch my breath. I grabbed my friend, he was about to die. He told me, "Don't waste your life. You're special. Be somebody!" Tears filled my eyes and I begged him to hold on! He was the big brother I never had. But God had other plans, and he died with my arms wrapped around him, as if I could shelter him from death. But there was nothing I could do.

Now I can't explain what I was feeling in that moment,

because it was a sensation that you really can't explain. After it was all over, I didn't even hear anything else, and in my mind all I could see were only the bloody faces of my friends. They had all died.

My friend grabbed a bag of drugs from the car and we started to run. I ran and ran and ran. I was scared, I was tired, and I was dying inside my soul. But, when I looked up I was alone. No friend.

No drug bag.

I was alone.

And I didn't know where I was.

The sun was almost rising, I slowed down, but I kept on moving. Soon, I got to another town; it was about 7:00 AM. I rested myself next to a door, I sat, and then I put my head down.

Soon after that I felt someone touch my shoulder. It was a man. He asked me, "Are you okay?"

I didn't answer.

"I can help you."

"NO!" I practically screamed, "No one can help me!"

He looked at me with great compassion in his eyes. "Come with me."

"What?"

I don't know why, but I decided to go with him in his car. As soon as I rested my head on the comfortable seat, I was sound asleep. When I woke up, I was on a bed. The first thing that came to my mind was that this was all a dream.

But then, I figured out that it couldn't be a dream. I got up and I walked out of the room. Right outside of my room sat the person who helped me. He was a priest. When he saw me he told me, "Don't be worried, son. I only want to help you."

"Where I am I?"

"You are in a seminary. If you want, you can stay here. You will be safe."

I was still confused, and I didn't know what to do so I didn't answer right away. I stayed there for a few weeks, and I told him what had happened to me. That priest and the other fathers helped me with my problems.

It is truly incredible how your life can change from one day to another.

I hate to think about what would have happened if I was in that car with my friends. I guess I would have died too. Was it luck that saved me? I don't think so! Was this a thing of destiny? I don't know! The only thing that I know for sure is that I am glad to be alive and that I had the chance to turn my life around.

I want to thank all the good people who helped me: my mother, my father, my brothers, my sisters, my friends, and all the people who helped me to change my life.

Even now, sometimes when I remember all these things I have seen in my life, my eyes fill with tears and I can't hold the pain in. I want to cry but I don't do it. The world is made for strong people and I don't want to cry. I want to survive in this world and be somebody important in this life. I have to be strong and never look back - never go back. What I hold in my heart is my dream, and it gives me energy and wisdom to go on to realize that dream.

The dream of helping the ones like me who have a hard life.

The dream of helping all my "HOMIES" in Mexico so they don't waste their lives, or worse yet, **lose** their lives.

We were meant to be strong men and good men.

Let us be it.

The DREAM.

When you come to the end of all the light you know, and it's time to step into the darkness of the unknown, faith is knowing that one of two things shall happen: Either you will be given something solid to stand on or you will be taught to fly.

- Edward Teller

Victor Palillero is seventeen years old. He is an ESL student in Lindenwold High School. His aspirations for the future involve bilingual psychology. In that future he hopes to help young people make their lives better, to make better choices for themselves, to have better thinking skills and decision making skills, which will provide those who use them a better way of life for not only themselves, but for the ones they love.

The meaning of life is to give life meaning.

- Ken Hudgins

The Written Works of
Yeni Rodriguez

I Was a Little Flower…

I was a little flower dropped on the ground
I was a little butterfly who flew all around;
I was a quiet voice hidden from harm
I was a sobbing child in my mother's arms
I have been many things, each new
Changing and growing
Yet never sure of myself
Never sure of what or who I was.

Now, I am the flower, looking at the sun
The butterfly focuses when the day is done
My voice is not afraid to tell the truth now
The child no longer hides in fear or bows
I have been many things, each new
Trusting and caring
Always being sure of myself
Always sure of who I am and what I want

Yeni M. Rodriguez is a seventeen-year-old student at Lindenwold High School. She is a very bright ESL student who came from Honduras to the U.S. in November of 2002. Her goals are to graduate from high school, attend a university, and became a professional person later in life. Yeni enjoys going to church and playing soccer. We all wish her much luck in the future!

The purpose of life, after all, is to live it, to taste experience to the utmost, to reach out eagerly and without fear for newer and richer experiences.

- Eleanor Roosevelt

The Written Works of
Sarafina Muhammad

True Love?

True Love is what I wanted
True Love is what he gave me
Or so I thought
He said he would wait for me
But he didn't
And he took my heart right along with him
I remember the way he touched my face, my heart,
my soul
Now
He's far away from me
He's gone
And it's okay
I have learned my lesson
True love will still find me
Because my heart is good
But
It will never find him

Never!

Everyday

Everyday I pray
that you won't go away

Everyday I cry
Trying not
to tell a lie

Every night I wish
You were here
holding me tight.

…Every night.

You must have long term
goals to keep you from
being frustrated by short term failures.

- Charles C. Noble

Sarafina is a sixteen-year-old sophomore at Lindenwold High School. Her hobbies are: talking on the
phone, eating, and shopping. Oh, yes… and writing!
Her family consists of: her loving mom, Ameena, a
brother named Idriys, and, the love of her life, her ten-
month-old son, Shaheem.

Our greatest battles are that
with our own minds.

- Jameson Frank

The Written Works of
Madalyn Natividad

The Star that Wouldn't Fall

I am lost in both time and space
your face is fading from its place
like a struggle between two maniac minds
fractures and fine lines will pave the way
it's so hard not to break thin ice on such a hot day
making my heart drop lower, deeper in my chest
pounding harder, dying to rest
too troubled to speak; my bones feel weak
I am scared as you draw me deeper, closer into your stare
no matter how much I wish I may, I wish I might
I know I could never make you mine tonight
yet I stand with you and am mesmerized by your every move
I cannot say which is worse
teasing me or cutting you from the scene
well to this life and to this love we are cursed
why did this have to happen
while we are so young
with so much to know and so much to learn
we were so in love and so naive
I did not know yet which things I believed
thinking back if I could ever have been perfect
I would have been perfect for you
but for all we've been through, we've gotten pretty far
if I let you go tonight, it would be hard
not knowing how I would scar
I am tired yet sleepless
'cause when I dream, I dream of you and I won't lie
tonight the stars have your name written across the sky
I reach to knock them down but they are far too high
my mirror has painted your picture so
clearly next to my reflection

more and more you spread through my body like an infection
I know in all of this
I'm completely outrageous
like something contagious enough for medication
in photo albums of my blood shot eyes
lay scratched out captions
nervous as I confess
they were written in words of regret and stupid actions

Love takes off masks that we fear we cannot live without and know we cannot live within.

- James Baldwin

Madalyn "Maddie" Natividad is a talented fifteen-year-old writer. Maddie loves to write (obviously) and she loves to play soccer.

After high school she hopes to attend a media arts university in Florida. Maddie's bigger plans are to become a T.V. news journalist. We are sure she will become a huge success in whatever she chooses to do!

Nothing great in the world has ever
been accomplished without passion.

The Written Works of
Ian Brown

Lost In Translation

Many people come and go
And most of them we just don't know
They have unfamiliar faces and come
from even more unfamiliar places
They have different customs
and different meanings
And you may be offended
by their feelings
Because most strangers
are misunderstood
And Lost In Translation

Poetry

It can be mysterious
It can be SCARY
It can be funny
It can be sharing
Perhaps a thing of all
feelings and themes
Poetry is much, much
more than it seems
It might rhyme
It might take no time
To compose Poetry is art
And believe me it comes
straight from the heart
It's different from every culture
Poetry is altered but has
a root of nature
It may be a lot of things
But its importance is
unrivaled by anything
It has a flow about it, *Floetry*
It is the infinite potential
we all call Poetry.

You are always in my heart.
You are not alone. You are not alone.
Say it again. You are not
alone. You are not alone.
Not Alone, Not Alone.
You just reach out for me girl, in
the mornin', in the evenin'
Not alone. Not alone. You and Me,
Not Alone. Together, together.
You are never alone.

- A quote from the genius of Michael Jackson

Ian Brown is a sophomore at Lindenwold High School. He is a talented writer with a genuine feel for his poetry. He is also funny, bright, and has a heart of gold. Upon graduation Ian plans to attend Princeton University and aspires to one day get his Doctorate. Whatever his plans, he is SURE to succeed!

The difference between can and
cannot are only three letters.
Three letters that determine
your life's direction.

The Written Works of
Brionna Scotton

If Only

If only you'd look at me
I'd never want to blink
Because that would make you
disappear from my eyes
And I'd never want to miss
the sight of you

If only you'd smile at me
My world would be brighter
My heart would be filled with joy
And I'd be happy for the rest of my life

If only you'd talk to me
I'd listen intently to your every word
And I'd never interrupt you
when you'd speak
So I could always hear your voice

If only all these things would come to pass
I'd be surrounded by happiness
But for right now, I watch you
Wondering
"If only…"

That One Thing

I've never had the courage to say
The one thing that I've longed to tell you
Three simple words that aren't so simple

It's always so easy
To tell friends and family
But to tell you, the one I adore
It's way too difficult

I want to tell you
But if I do -- what would you do
Tell me the words I've longed to hear
Or tell me you don't feel the same

My heart is on my sleeve
Waiting for you to take hold of it
But the question for you is:
Will you keep it or will you throw it away

The question for me is:
Will I ever have the courage to tell you?
To *say* that one thing I've *never* been able to?
To tell you…

"I love you."

It only takes one person to
change your life – you.

- Ruth Casey

Brionna Scotton is fifteen years old. Her birthday is April 30th. Brionna likes to read and write stories – both short and long. She plays field hockey and softball and has joined many clubs at Lindenwold High School: The Leo Club, The Ski and Adventure Club, The LHS Dance Team, and now, The Teen Writers Guild! She always strives to *do* and *be* her best! Ms. Scotton's favorite class is Chemistry, her second favorite is English. Brionna lives at home with her mother and two siblings, Jo and Michael, and cousin, Steven. She is also the proud owner of a four-year-old dog named Handsome, and a cute cat named Tigger.

When you make a mistake, don't look back at it long. Take the reason of the thing into your mind and then look forward. Mistakes are lessons of wisdom. The past cannot be changed. The future is yet in your power.

- Hugh White

The Written Works of
Karla Siete

Admiration

I walked into class and my teacher said, "Tell me who you admire the most." First, I thought about my aunt, but I did not immediately realize that I had chosen the wrong person. Then, I started thinking again. I was in English class with my favorite teacher. But the thing is that she was not just my *favorite* teacher; she also was a special person in my life.

Her name is Mrs. Mosley-Duffy.

She has so many excellent qualities; it is impossible to pick only a few.

Mrs. Mosley-Duffy is a great teacher. She teaches me many things that I will never forget. She is one of my biggest inspirations.

I think, sometimes, for me, it is very difficult to explain how much I admire her. Some of her best characteristics are: she is nice, understanding, and trustworthy. I can say that it's really hard to find a wonderful teacher like her. She might not be the only one, but she might be one of the few that are left. Besides this, she is a diamond that maybe can never be found again. She is a sweet person who shows her love and likes to give you advice, as a loving mother would do.

Even though she is a teacher, she is also a good friend. She is the friend that everyone would like to have.

Mrs. Mosley is a responsible person and she is always there when I need her. She always cares about others. Mrs. Mosley is a funny teacher, but at the same time she is very strict with her students, not because she hates them, but because she cares about them. When I walk in the hallways, sometimes I feel that she is behind me calling out, "Hi, Karla! How are you? How is your family doing?"

Concluding all this, I think Mrs. Mosley-Duffy is a wonderful person who I will never forget.

And I will always admire her … for the rest of my life.

Karla Siete is eighteen years old. She is a senior at Lindenwold High school. She is originally from El Salvador. Miss Siete is a wonderful person who likes to help all of her friends. Karla hopes to graduate with honors and then go to college after she graduates in 2007. She loves many sports: soccer, volleyball, basketball… Finally, she plans to have her own drywall business after she graduates from college. In the future, Karla wants to help many kids from other countries and to also make herself and those children proud to be who they are.

We don't know who we are until
we see what we can do.

- Martha Grimes

The Written Works of
Brittany Alston

Me Without You

I placed my all in you
But you took advantage of me
I gave everything to you
But you neglected me

Enough
is
Enough!

I could only take but so much
I guess you don't agree, because
now you want me, huh?
So, I want you to tell me what's changed?
I am still me
and you're still you
Tell me why
WHY?
I loved you **soooooo** much
Wasn't that enough?
Oh, *I* see now
You thought I would stick around…
Now you want what you can't have
You want what you *once* had
It doesn't work like that
Let me tell you how things work
Reality must start setting in for you
I am gone

WE has become a you and a me
You're confused?!
Why?
Me and you, we're through
I loved you, but now I love me
I gave my all to you
Now I give all of myself to me
I am free of your problems, your pettiness
I am learning who I am
I can't love you if I don't know me
Now you want all of this, **but** I can't give it to you

I am the only one who controls my heart beat
I am being responsibly selfish now,
The shoes have changed feet
I am hogging my intelligence, my love, my life
I want no part of your strife

You weren't enough

You see how it feels?
It hurts, doesn't it?

Well…

That's tough

A real friend is someone who walks in
when the rest of the world walks out

- Anon.

Brittany Alston is a sixteen-year-old from Lindenwold, New Jersey. She is proud to be a member of The Teen Writers Guild of Lindenwold High School. Brittany enjoys writing about issues that affect her personally. Brittany also loves to listen to different genres of music and spend time with her friends and family. She takes her school work very seriously. Ms. Alston wants to continue her education by going to undergraduate and graduate schools. Brittany Alston is a determined and motivated young adult – a shining example of how hard work pays off in so many wonderful ways!

All your life you are told the things you cannot do. All your life they will say you're not good enough or strong enough or talented enough; they will say you're the wrong height or the wrong weight or the wrong type to play this or be this or achieve this. THEY WILL TELL YOU NO, a thousand times no, until all the no's become meaningless. All your life they will tell you no, quite firmly and very quickly.
AND THEN, YOU WILL
TELL THEM YES!!!

- Nike AD

The Written Works of
Britt Robertson

What Do You Do Then?

Will the pain ever go away?
Why does it linger
and stay
It happened in the *past*
There's nothing that can be done about it
So why do these issues continue to last?
I want to get over it
Move on with my life
And yet, they're still holding me back
Randomly throwing my brain out of whack
Distraught and torn up inside
I am constantly on an emotional ride
I need to be at peace
To say the least
They say, "Express your feelings!"
"Don't keep things bottled up inside!"
But what if you can't?
What if that's not even an option?

What do you do then?

It was when...

It was when my whole world
came tumbling down
When my wonderful life shattered to pieces
When my deepest darkest
secret rose to the surface
When the hidden molestation of my
past came out of darkness
When the flashbacks from so long
ago broke my heart again
It was when I couldn't tell anyone
When I was too afraid to tell my parents
When I knew my sisters wouldn't understand
When my family just couldn't handle it.
When I confided in my friends but
they didn't know what to say
When they wanted to help but
they didn't know how
It was when I had no one else in the world

That was when I put trust in GOD
That was when I opened the good book
That was when I referred to my Bible
When I sought guidance further than man
That was when I started praying and believing
When I put all faith in God
That was when I *faced* my issues
instead of running away from them
When Jesus was all I had
That was when I found out…
He was all I ever needed.

When Jesus was all you had,
that's when you realized
HE is all you've ever needed.

- Rev. Keith Garland

Britt Robertson is a young Christian lady. Britt is very short but ironically she **loves** basketball! Her interests are sneaker shopping, stuntin' shades, church, all sports, and just hangin' out. In her chill time she's very goofy, but, when she's serious, you might just want to step off! Britt's goals are to be Valedictorian in 2009 and then to attend Princeton where she will major in child psychology.

Most of the important things in the world have been accomplished by people who have kept on trying when there seemed to be no hope at all.

- Dale Carnegie

The Written Works of
Gregory Forest

Imagine
(a fictional tale)

Imagine being a child from an affair
your father committed
Imagine being the only child with no friends
Imagine you and your mother living on the street
Imagine being just ten pounds at two years old
Imagine eating trash and drinking water from the sewer
Imagine crying your eyes out
Imagine your father not being there for you
Imagine being cold in the winter and
being too hot in the summer
Imagine your mom being an escort to
get money for clothes and food
Imagine kids from school making fun of you
Imagine getting into fights everyday
because they're teasing you
Imagine getting pregnant when you're just fifteen years old
Imagine your boyfriend abandoning you and your baby
Imagine living the same life your mother lived
Imagine working at Burger King to
support you and your baby
Imagine meeting your father for the first time
Imagine you father saying "Sorry" and hugging you

What would *you* do?
How would *you* feel?
What would you say?
What *could* you say?!

Gregory Forest is sixteen years old and a Junior at Lindenwold High School. His hobbies are: golf, writing books, and video games. He lives at home with his mother, Pamela, his father, Gregory Sr., brother, Tony, and a sweet, friendly, dog named Leo. Gregory has embraced his part in The Teen Writers Guild and his fellow Guild Members enjoy him as a person, as well as his work!

We must have a theme, a goal, a purpose in our lives. If you don't know where you're aiming, you don't have a goal. My goal is to live my life in such a way that when I die, someone can say, she cared.

- Mary Kay Ash

The Written Works of
Desiree' Forrest

My Struggle

Ecstatic
Melancholy
My ups
My downs
The Sex...
Rape
He took it
I'm scared now
Pregnancy no
So condoms
Forever
Rumors/my rep
The Violence...
One step
The gun
I picked it up
I put it down
The knife/despair
She was stabbed
Remorse for her
My heart didn't care
The Family...
The lies
Half truths
Never whole
Real father
Not him
Eviction
Broken home
We left

He stalked
The stalking subsided
The Drugs...
Prime example
Marijuana
I fight it
2 a.m.
I'm giddy
I'm laughing
Eyes red
They're glazed
I smoke it
Simply to hide my fears
The Pain...
They lied
Lost hope
Broken hearts
Lost love
Suicide
The cuts
I'm torn apart
The wounds
I hide them
Do they show?
I don't know
The Truth...
My life
The depth
Where did it go?
The pain
Still remains
My death?

Is it near?
I'm scared
Out loud
I'm crying out tears
Help?
Do I want it?
No, I'll figure it out

Was I the real me before the pain and the suffering?
Or am I me now...after the struggling?

Your life will be no better than the plans you make and the action you take. You are the architect and builder of your own life, fortune, and destiny.

- Alfred A. Montapert

Holding anger is a poison. It eats you from inside. We think that hating is a weapon that attacks the person who harmed us. But hatred is a curved blade. And the harms we do, we do to ourselves.

- Mitch Albom

Desiree' Forrest was born and raised in Lindenwold, N.J. She was born on August 21, 1989 and is now a senior in Lindenwold High School. Her hobbies include urban novel writing, acting, and music. Desiree' plans to attend Camden County College in the fall of 2007 to receive her degree in Small Business Operations. Her ultimate goal is to become a proprietor/ well-known urban novelist. So far she has written four unpublished novels, and has great hopes for her future. And, **we** have great hopes for her, too!

How do I change?

If I feel depressed I will sing.
If I feel sad I will laugh.
If I feel ill I will double my labor.
If I feel fear I will plunge ahead.
If I feel inferior I will wear new garments.
If I feel uncertain I will raise my voice.
If I feel poverty I will think
of wealth to come.
If I feel incompetent I will
think of past success.
If I feel insignificant I will
remember my goals.
Today I will be the master of my emotions.

- Og Mandino

The Written Works of
Makepeace Cotto

MY DADDY

Daddy... ???
That word doesn't even exist for me
Growing up was hard
And I wish you were around but now I see
You are not special to me
You are a fool
Afraid to be the father I needed as a seed
No one knows what it's like not having you with
me
When I most needed you
You were never to be found
I called your wife
She would tell me go away
Do you know the tears I shed?
Did you care that my heart was broken?
The answer is no
And, for a while, the world shut down on me
I felt small
I felt alone
What kind of man doesn't want his own
daughter?
No real man, that's for sure
I was sick and you didn't care
I was in the hospital and needed a kidney
You were my only hope
and my cure

But all you did was make me worse
My saving grace?
My prayers made it through
and yes
<u>HE</u> heard me
I am better off without you
I stand tall all on my own
So if you expect *me* to call *you* Daddy
Think again
Daddy is the man who raises you
not the boy who conceives you
But it's all good
Because even though you were never here
to nurture me and to help me grow
I'm grown and I'm smart
Smart enough to know who MY DADDY is
And one thing I know for sure
MY DADDY will NEVER be you!

It doesn't matter who my
father was; it matters who
I remember he was.

- Ann Sexton

Makepeace Cotto is fifteen years old. Makepeace currently attends Lindenwold High School and is in the 10th grade. She is dedicated to her school work and tries to get involved in many school activities. Makepeace enjoys writing. She loves to express herself in words so people can read about what she is going through. Makepeace has been writing since she was eleven years old. Growing up was hard for her and she didn't know another way to release pain, so she would write! Makepeace likes to sing, dance, meet new people, have fun, and just be herself. Makepeace hopes you enjoy her writing. Miss Cotto also hopes that she inspires you to write and become a poet because really, everyone is a poet in their heart. To write, is to be free.

Readers are plentiful; thinkers are rare.

- Harriet Martineau

The Written Works of
Symone Robinson

Imagination

I wish I had time to relax
Time to think
Time to look back
I want to close my eyes
Let it sink in
I want to take a deep breath
And use my imagination

I want to dream
That's how I stop the complication
You know life is not at all what it seems
I need to breathe and be free
To just be me
And use my imagination

I wish the world was different
It's time to think
Time to listen
Let it sink in
Take a deep breath
Close your eyes

Just dream
Yes, life isn't at all what it seems
But I could slip into my mind's creation
If I could just be me
and breathe
Then
I would be free
To sit and use my imagination.

Symone Robinson is a fifteen-year-old honor student who loves her friends very much. She loves writing, and misses her dead chicken, Paublo. She also likes her buddy, Pelle Greeno's purple pants. Symone also enjoys eating, watching T.V., and playing with Justin Terry's hair. Miss Robinson is a very interesting soul, to say the least.

There are many things we do not want
about the world. Let us not just mourn
them. Let us change them.

- Ferdinand Marcos

The Written Works of
Bonvincent Hernandez

Discovering Life

As I look into the sky,
I see beyond the backlit mountain range.
I see beyond the jagged edges of my
snowcapped view.
I see further than all of the mountain climbers
and their adventurous treks.
I see life.
I realize all the beauty and emotion through
the sky and its azure.
I realize all the obstacles and barriers to come
through the unpredictable ridges.
And I realize all the ups and downs through
the climbers.
I see my whole life right before my eyes.

I'm Waiting

I'm waiting for that special someone,
someone that makes life sweet.
Not waiting for my rocket to come,
just waiting for the girl that knocks me off my feet.

It's not all about looks or style,
or anything of that kind.
One thing that she has to have,
Is a positive mind.
I often find myself alone,
Wondering without a clue.
When this girl is going to come,
And what am I to do.

I just need that one girl you see,
I don't want to have to end up making a choice.
Though once I find her,
I'll wait by the phone every night
longing to hear her voice.

One day she'll come I tell you,
Just you wait and see.
And when that day comes,
My life will be complete.

Only those who risk going too far
can possibly find out how far one can go.

- T.S. Eliot

Bonvincent Hernandez is one of many students at Lindenwold High School (Class of '09). He lives with his parents. His family originally comes from the Philippines. Mr. Hernandez enjoys playing sports, participating in band, and tries to help others as much as he can. He is deeply involved as a student. Bonvincent is part of the bowling team, marching band, indoor drumline, LEO Club, and Student Government. He is also a volunteer teacher for religious education. For all his involvement, Bonvincent is a laid-back person who loves to have a good time in everything he does. (And he does!)

The harder the conflict, the more glorious the triumph. What we obtain too cheap, we esteem too lightly; it is dearness only that gives everything its value. I love the man that can smile in trouble, that can gather strength from distress and grow brave by reflection. 'Tis the business of little minds to shrink; but he whose heart is firm, and whose conscience approves his conduct, will pursue his principles unto death.

- Thomas Paine

The Written Works of
Anna Kriner

He Was Never Really There

Her name was Kathleen, born on May nineteenth

He was the happiest man and too excited to sleep

He washed her, clothed her, and fed her until she was happy

He loved her more than life itself and gave everything up just for her and her health

She was in the hospital three or four times, but the doctor said she would be just fine

Little did he know this sweet baby, wasn't going to be the woman they were hoping she would be

At only three months old, God wanted her back and she heard the call

Kathleen died in her sleep

We did nothing that day, but cry and weep

It was the worst day, but we all got through

Except for someone, it was a little harder to do

Nothing worked, not psychology, not even Al-Anon

So instead he went the wrong road and went to a bad town

He wasn't thinking right, he just wasn't himself

So he left, and went the wrong way instead of getting help

He was in Camden, getting high off the oxycontin

While his wife's at home and his family's hitting rock bottom

He skipped out on his job so they don't make any dough

What's he gonna do?

He's got two kids to show.

that he really loves to death and for them...

he would take his last breath

He really doesn't know how much it hurt everybody to see him like that

A 32 year-old man getting high and then trying to cut back and when he did...

He just couldn't resist.

He had to go do it again and take that risk...

Of losing his family, of losing his wife, but he didn't care about anyone

Only his own life

He almost got killed roaming the streets, and called his house pleading for somewhere to sleep

He wasn't disowned, he was my brother again, but something wasn't right...

It just wasn't him

I have a drugged up brother, it hurts for me to say

But what am I supposed to do?

He goes his own way...

I hope he knows that I'll love him until the day I die...

No matter what he does, I'll be by his side

So this is for you, my brother who I love

I hope you stop doing those drugs

In loving memory of Kathleen Charlotte Kriner

05.19.04 - 09.02.04

The salvation of this human world lies nowhere else than in the human heart, in the human power to reflect, in human meekness and human responsibility.

- Vaclav Havel

Anna Kriner is fourteen years old and lives with her parents and two brothers. She believes that writing is therapeutic and hopes that others will pick up a pen and learn the tremendous healing power when one learns how to express themselves.

If I were asked to give what I consider the single most useful bit of advice for all humanity, it would be this: Expect trouble as an inevitable part of life, and when it comes, hold your head high, look it squarely in the eye, and say, "I will be bigger than you. You cannot defeat me."

- Ann Landers

The Written Works of
Megan Herrera

FREE

So soft and kind
I see your face inside my head
Recollecting all the memories of you
My admiration was easily fed.
Crying in the shame of being mislead
Concluding everything you said was
completely untrue
My soft image of you was instantly dead.
I was forced to think you were God.
Offspring are given expectations to meet.
You made me weak
So I never fought.
It came to my advantage to lie and cheat.
Now I'm alone
And you're against me
It's time for me to step up
And become

FREE.

Megan Herrera attends Lindenwold High School. She is involved with many activities, but drama is her all time favorite. Megan is happiest while spending time with her best friend, Kaitlyn Kopec. She will eventually go to college and try to pursue her dream to become a well-known film critic. AND... a few of Megan's favorite films???

...White Oleander, Selena, Rent, and Dirty Dancing.

Throw away those books and cassettes on inspirational leadership. Send those consultants packing. Know your job, set a good example for the people under you and put results over politics. That's all the charisma you'll really need to succeed.

- Dyan Machan

The Written Works of
Rob DiClementi

At the Old Ball Game

Nothing gets fans more excited than a good old-fashioned rivalry. When the Yankees and Red Sox clash, it isn't your ordinary rivalry.

When you judge two teams you have to consider the amount of talent they have and you have to think about the past as well. The Yanks have won, count them, 26 World Series. The Boston Red Sox have won only one since 1918. Give me a break. Even until late, the Red Sox have only beat the Yankees in the playoffs once, on a fluke set of games. The Yanks have just murdered the Sox in the playoffs. Aaron Boone anybody? How about Bucky Dent? These players are true Red Sox killers. The Red Sox should be the definition of choke.

This year it's obvious that the Yankees will remain the champions of the AL East. Their team is much better than the Red Sox. They improved their line-up in a huge way by adding former Red Sox centerfielder Johnny Damon. He was the face of the Red Sox for years and the Yanks are glad to get him. A Sox loss always seems to be a Yankees gain. I expect big things from the Yankee line-up. Every position seems to be close, if not better than the Red Sox. Both teams are going to score a ton of runs, but the Yankees are going to score many more.

Let's face it, everyone was happy that the Red Sox won their first World Series. They are not constantly expected to win the whole thing every year. If the Yankees don't make the World Series, it is an off year. There is no bigger pressure than playing a game under the highest pedestal in Yankee Stadium. The pressures of playing a season as a New York Yankee are immense. If you succeed in your play, you will be forever remembered. That is the difference between the Yanks and the Sox.

You either love or hate the owner of the Yankees, George Steinbrenner. There is no in between. He is willing to do anything to win, and that is a commitment I think every owner should have. The more money you spend, the better the product you put on the field is going to be. Like the saying goes, "You have to spend money to make money."

Just to think about what the ballpark has seen and the people that have walked through is remarkable. Just being in the same stadium that Joe DiMaggio, Lou Gehrig, Babe Ruth, and Mickey Mantle played in is truly an honor. When I went to Yankee Stadium last year I looked at the field and pondered. I thought about Lou Gehrig making his remarkable speech even in the face of the terrible disease with which he was stricken. I thought about "Mr. October", Reggie Jackson cranking three homeruns in a World Series game and Roger Maris belting his 61st homerun to right field. I get chills when I go back to think about it. Nothing against Fenway Park, but it can not touch Yankee Stadium.

Throughout the decades, they have kept a commitment to winning. The fans will always be there, no matter how good or bad they are doing. Being at a Yankees game is like nothing else you can ever do. You can see how much the fans care about the team. The crowd is nuts, but you can't touch the excitement of a Yankees fan when they are about to play the Sox, whether they are home or at Fenway.

Adversity cause some men to break; others to break records.

- William Ward

Rob DiClementi is a fifteen-year-old sophomore. He was born in Philadelphia, Pa., on April 28th, 1991. Rob is an only child, lovingly raised by Barbara and Dominic DiClementi. Rob's goals in life are to become a renowned journalist for a top national newspaper, to become a responsible adult, and to raise a good family of his own someday.

Mourn not the dead that in the cool earth lie, but rather mourn the apathetic throng, the cowed and the meek who see the world's great anguish and its wrong, and dare not speak!

- Ralph Chaplin

The Written Works of
Diana Casas

THE LAST DAY

"He didn't want to go away." He said.
"My little baby is going to suffer a lot
because she can't understand anything.
I want to stay. I want to stay."
Those were my father's last words.
Then, everything changed.
Nothing went back to be the same as before.
The tree was cut and fell down to sleep forever.
I saw many people around me. It was
like a party. Some women were cooking a
lot of food and the house smelled of
mole. Also, the vultures were happy because
for them this day was one they had
waited long for. The dogs howled like
they had lost somebody from their
own family. After that, I heard the band
playing music like in a Cinderella
movie. People were strange with black
clothing. As well, I saw a gray box over a
table and around it were four big candles.
The people stood watching me and all
the flowers were sad. I couldn't understand
anything, it was like a volcano that
wanted to explode inside of me, but my
mother later described that day as if
heaven was falling down over her. Also,
I wanted to run away, but I couldn't,
I was a tree rooted to the floor, not allowed
to leave. The stares spoke that they
really cared about us, but at the same time;

sadness. I heard my mom cry like a
wolf, but every time louder and louder. It
was like a hurricane that you never
knew when it was going to stop. Suddenly,
there was a long silence like the
ocean at night. Even my mother stopped
crying and fell down like a flower
without water, I felt a very hard pain in
my heart which stays with me even
today.
I saw a big hole and men were putting a
box into it. Then, they covered it
with soil and it became another little
mountain of soil like the other ones.
My heart left my body that day
and joined his in heaven.
The sad flowers
Two days later
Bent their heads down in pain.

Just when the caterpillar thought the world was over… it became a butterfly

Diana Elizabeth Casas Meneses is a sixteen-year-old young woman in ESL IV at Lindenwold High School. She is originally from México, and in the future she would like to study Tourism/travel. Diana lives with her mother and siblings. Sadly, her father died when she was only two years old. Diana is known to one and all as a very thoughtful, intelligent, and good friend.

The world is a dangerous place to live; not because of the people who are evil, but because of the people who don't do anything about it.

- Albert Einstein

The Written Works of
Abrianna Wilp-O'Neill

Second Glance

He is the one she really loves
He's the one; but in reality; he doesn't even know
she's there.
He doesn't know,
He doesn't even care.
She walks down the hallways,
Not once does he glance her way.
A new look; a new personality,
Head cheerleader; Prom Queen
Wow!! Look Now!!
There he is all over her,
She thought she'd like it.
Her lover, finally seeing her,
But now she's fake.
Just like all those other girls,
She didn't want to become.
New day, Same old girl
He doesn't even know that,
She's the girl that walks down the hallway.
Even now, without a second glance.

BEST FRIEND

The knife was her best friend.
but no one knew.
She told herself lies about why her hand was so red.
But no one knew.
She went to school
Lived her life.
but no one knew.
Just at night, when everyone was asleep
That's when her only best friend came out.
but no one knew
not even when
she was the last person
to see the red on her hand.

I cannot believe that the purpose of life is to be happy. I think the purpose of life is to be useful, to be responsible, to be compassionate. It is, above all to matter, to count, to stand for something, to have made some difference that you lived at all.

Abrianna Wilp-O'Neill or, as many call her, Abby, is a smart, pretty, sarcastic (at times), and athletic girl. She has a lot to accomplish in life and she is willing to put all of her heart into whatever comes her way. She loves having fun with her friends. Abrianna lives with her mom and little sister. Remember, people will judge you by your actions, not your intentions.

We can let circumstances rule
us, or we can take charge and
rule our lives from within.

- Earl Nightengale

The Written Works of
Cynthia Recarte

QUINCIANERA

The day is coming soon. I said the day is coming soon! So much emotion. So much excitement!

I was so thrilled. I woke up that morning hearing the song "La Pequena Nina". That day was special for me because my birthday had come! All my family was excited! I woke up early in the morning and I took a shower. Then, I and my parents went to the ballroom that we had rented. We spent all morning there decorating everything in orange and white. I love the color orange! It was very late. The girl that was supposed to do my hair was at home, but I wasn't there! I was running back and forth. My mom was yelling. She was crazy like me.

A lot of presents were in the living room piled as tall as a mountain. They were all mine of course! One was a big doll that would be my last doll of childhood. I started to cry because I now I was becoming a woman.

It was 4 o'clock and my hair was *still* not ready. My mother was very worried. Finally, the hairdressers arrived. After that, I saw my dress on the bed. It was so pretty, like a dream, large, flouncy, orange with many layers. It made me look like a princess. My quincianera was my dream come true. In our country, we call this a quincianera, but here in the U.S. they call it a "sweet sixteen". It's not the same. This is an amazing day with many rituals, lots of family and friends, and joy. There were fourteen young men to escort me into the ballroom. I received a necklace from my family and my last doll. From now on I would no longer be a child. We expressed our love to each other. At the party, we danced, ate food and we had fun all together.

Now, I am a woman.

ESL CLASS

Funny friends falling into the classroom
A pool of love
Splashing ideas and hopes and dreams
Always swimming fast to learn more
When things get difficult
We don't want to swim
We get out of the pool and go home
The next day
We dive in the deep end
And start another day

We don't know who we are until
we see what we can do.

Cynthia Recarte is seventeen years old. She is a Junior at Lindenwold High school. Ms. Recarte lives at home with her loving parents, Jose and Lorena Recarte, and her sisters: Loren, Stacy and Eliana.

The moment of recognizing your own lack of talent is a flash of genius.

- Stanislaw Jerzy Lem

The Written Works of
Ivan A. Pineiro

"**Thankful**" was written when Ivan was in 7th grade. (It is re-vamped a bit here) His feelings have not changed. They are still as sincere and heart-felt as they were back then.

Thankful

11/19/03

The thing I am most thankful for is my parents.

I am thankful for them because they brought me into this world - without them I wouldn't exist.

Another reason why I am thankful for them is because without them I wouldn't have food to eat and shelter to keep me out of the cold. They sacrifice for me, they care about the quality of my life and they care about the quality of my education.

I am also thankful for them because they are the ones who will always love and care for me.

My parents are very important to me.

For all of these reasons and so many more, my parents mean the world to me; and I am thankful for my parents because not only do I have people who love me, but I have people that I can love back.

Ivan Pineiero is a fifteen-year-old student who comes from a very loving and caring family. Ivan is an honor student who is working toward a bright future as a mechanical and structural engineer. He enjoys hanging out with his friends, playing sports, playing chess, and spending time with his family.

I think I should have no other mortal wants, if I could always have plenty of music. It seems to infuse strength into my limbs and ideas into my brain. Life seems to go on without effort, when I am filled with music.

- George Eliot (1819 - 1880)

The Written Works of
Jessica Kealey

There is an "I" in friendship

I spend all my time with the people
who pretend they're 'friends'.
The people who screw me over every chance they get.
The ones who say they care,
But when I need them, they aren't there.
This is how the relationship goes,
But I don't think it's what I chose.
Is it?
They always complain
And it's driving me insane.
But when something happens to me,
I try to make them see
They push me away and
I never get a chance to say--
All those people and the role they play...
What's 'friendship' anyway?
How'd it end up this way?
I miss being a kid and going out to play.
When did it go wrong?
Or did we know this all along?
Just give up and go away; I think I'm better off alone.
I give up; I'm sick of listening; I'm
putting my feelings on loan.
I really can't take this anymore
It's just such a bore.
Same deal, different day.
I'm not listening to anything you say.
All those people and the role they play...
What's 'friendship' anyway?
Friendship should be fun.

You know what? - I'm done.
I need to be appreciated.
This message - I hope you get it.
This show is such a tragedy.
I'm not gonna be another causality.
Now I'm taking over.
The show's over.

For every man there comes that special
moment when he is offered the chance
to do a very special thing - unique
to him and fitted to his talents.
What a tragedy if that moment finds
him unprepared or unqualified for the
work which would be his finest hour.

Jessica Ann Kealey is just about the coolest girl you can meet. She's lived on the same dead-end street in Lindenwold all her life. She's laid-back with a quirky sense of humor. Her hobbies include: stage crew, listening to music, going to shows, concerts, spending time with her friends, The Leo Club, The French Club, reading, writing, and long walks on the beach! You'll never see her go two days without surfing the Internet, five minutes without taking out her cell phone, or EVER caught without a cd in her bag.

Anyone who lives within their means
suffers from a lack of imagination.

- Oscar Wilde

The Written Works of
Tashae Smith

When I Was Innocent

At age fourteen, I was known as the cute, smart, and innocent girl everybody protected. I was called 'Church Girl' and corny because I never went to parties or drank and smoked.

A powerful rage swept over me and turned me into a different person. I was tired of being known as innocent and smart to all my friends and family. So, I started drinking and smoking with drug dealers and going to parties and clubs.

It was fun while it lasted.

I started to see everybody with a boyfriend and girlfriend all cuddled up and loving each other. I was on a hunt but it didn't work out. Boys my age weren't really into "big girls" it seems. But there was a "party line" called The Loop. I had heard my cousins met some cute boys from there. So, I called it and that's where I met my boyfriend.

His name was Mike. We met in person after a couple of months. When I first saw him I liked him right away.

And, better yet, he liked me.

He was the kind of guy I dreamed about marrying. He was 5'10", caramel complexion, muscular, and fine!

He was also twenty-two years old.

When he first said he was twenty-two, I was quiet. I guess I should have listened to the silence. Mike would come over to my house and we chilled and everything was all good. About a month after chillin' and having fun he asked me to be his girl and me being young and not thinking of what this was really all about, I said, "yes."

One night he came over to hang out and he told me he loved me.

So I told him I loved him, too.

That night we made "Love".

I knew he had to be the one for me even though he was twenty-two and I was just fourteen. How crazy is that?

The next night he came back over, and we did it again.

Not long after that, I found out I was pregnant.

I told him about it and at first he said it was going to be okay, and that he wanted me to move in with him. Then he said to tell my mom, but I wanted to wait a while.

I guess I was scared.

Then things started to change and the man I gave my heart and body to decided he wasn't going to take care of anything.

My heart was destroyed and I felt sick. What kind of man is this? He says he loves me, and there's a baby, and then he so easily walked away accepting no responsibility at all.

This wasn't love.

This was just sex.

What a sad lesson to learn.

So, with no other choice, I told my parents about everything.

They made me get an abortion.

I was very depressed about it. Well, actually, I was very depressed about everything.

Then, out of the blue he called me up again, and I was so foolish that I allowed us to get back together, but it didn't last.

Apparently I didn't learn my sad lesson very well.

I know I'm not the only girl in the world who gave their innocence to the wrong person even though that's the way it feels. I'm sixteen now and I know I'm certain why a man almost ten years older than me wanted me so bad. He didn't just want me for my beauty, or that I might make a nice wife someday.

NO!

He wanted me for what I had control of...my innocence.

It was a power trip for him, a conquest, and sex.

That's not love.

Too bad sometimes it takes so many wrong things to show us the way to what's right.

I learned that it is the weak who are cruel, and that gentleness is to be expected only from the strong.

- Leo Rosten

Tashae is a lovely sixteen-year-old young lady attending Lindenwold High School. Tashae enjoys expressing her feelings through writing. She hopes that she encourages other young ladies in a positive way through her stories and poems. Tashae is a joy to be around and has a very sweet spirit. When Tashae graduates she hopes to be licensed as a registered nurse, and have a side career as a portrait model.

I can accept failure, but I
cannot accept not trying!

- Michael Jordan

The Written Works of
Bhagyesh Nayi

The World is a Bystander

Do you think bystanders shape history?

I think so, because they let history and events take place.

Professor Ervin Staub's theory states that bystanders who witness, but are not directly affected by, the actions of perpetrators, help shape society by their actions and through their inactions. I believe that his theory is true because bystanders can either stop events from happening or they can let them happen which genuinely affects society.

Albert Einstein said, "The world is a scary place, not because of the people that commit evil, it's the people that let evil happen."

During the holocaust, German society was a bystander. The hundreds of thousands of Germans who weren't involved in the war, could have helped to stop it.
Instead, they didn't do anything out of fear that they would be killed. They were silent during the whole war and didn't do a single thing, even when they could. If the German society took action and did something to stop the war, then the holocaust would not have been as bad as it was. The numbers of people killed would have decreased and there would have been *many* people around to live their lives, marry, raise families, and to tell the story of what they had experienced.

I also feel that young people these days are bystanders, also. If the kids know that there is going to be a fight in the school, they can either let it happen, or prevent it from happening. If the students let it happen, they are saying to others that there is nothing wrong with the violence. If they prevent it from happening, then they are trying to say that it is wrong to fight – and it is wrong.

However, some kids, as well as their parents just might not want to get into other people's business. Another example is young adults voting. That is a big way that young people can shape history. By voting, the people are shaping history because their vote counts and will determine who will be elected.

Many people feel as if they cannot make a difference. So they put out no effort.

But that's the wrong way to think. We <u>need</u> to be involved. We <u>must</u> stand up for what is right, decent, and moral.

To do anything else is to be a bystander.
And what can anyone ever accomplish by being that?

Motivation is everything.

- Lee Iacocca

Bhagyesh Nayi is a fifteen-year-old member of the Teen Writers Guild.

He was born in India and came to America when he was very young. He still holds much love in his heart for his native land.

Bhagyesh likes to play sports, write, and meet new people. Upon graduation, he hopes to attend a good local community college and then move on to Rutgers where he can get a degree in Business. Whatever he does in life, at work, *or* personally, he wants to be happy and successful. We are sure he will be all of *that* and then some!

And in the end....

You may have tangible wealth untold:
Caskets of jewels and coffers of gold.
But richer than I you can never be –
For I had a Mother who read to me.

- Strickland Gillilan

Personal note from Author Judith Kristen:

When Education Specialist, Genevieve Lumia asked me if I would like to start a Teen Writers Guild at Lindenwold High School, I immediately said, "YES!"

In less than a week I found myself sitting in the district office with Ms. Lumia and District Superintendent Geraldine Carroll discussing the Guild project I had completed at my old Alma Mater - Philadelphia's Frankford High School. That creation, a book entitled, "What We Want To Tell You", was an amazing success in so many ways! All three of us were filled with excitement and anticipation to recreate that success here in New Jersey. And so, by the end of our meeting, The Teen Writers Guild of Lindenwold High School was formed.

A week after that, I had a meeting with Lindenwold Principal, Frank Ranelli, his staff and many, many LHS teachers. We talked about the students: their need for creative expression, a desire to give a new voice to Lindenwold High, the pride in becoming published authors, and the long, worthwhile, and yet tough road through edits, rewrites, more rewrites, more edits, punctuation, rewrites, flow, cover creation, bios, galley proofs and ... did I mention *rewrites*?

Everyone agreed that this would be an outstanding project for these students, and best of all, so did the kids.

When I first visited Lindenwold students, it was during the first two days of school in September 2006. I was given forty-five minutes to speak to each assembly – there were four total. I told them a bit about my background, my work with The Teen Writers Guild of Frankford High School, and my passion for reading and writing.

Genevieve Lumia was with me on the second day, and, after my final assembly, we walked to the lunchroom together awaiting the students who would "Sign in, please", and join The Guild.

I honestly expected about 25 students.

Over 100 signed up!

Not only did they sign up to *write*, they signed on to help with the cover creation, the marketing of the book, to offer their computer skills, and *some* were even willing to help *others* edit and rewrite to assure that their friends' voices would be heard! Amazing!

Actually, the entire school became involved. Principal Ranelli would always ask me, "If there's anything we can do for you, consider it done!" Assistant Principal Leslie Betts-Woodward offered to share her office with me while I was working there; I accepted and we formed a terrific friendship. LHS teachers would stop me in the hallway or send me emails offering help to pull this book together. I'd like to thank educators extraordinaire: Ann Ryan, Tara Ringenwald, Kurt "Mr. D." DiGiovanni. Georganne Bubb, Joanne Porter, Marge Triplo, James Roddy, April Lee, Sam Rosetti, Robin Daniels, Laurie Scales, Larry Abrams, and Deborah Mosley-Duffy for all of their help and encouragement.

I also want to thank LHS staff members: Evelyn Hickman, Rachel McIntyre, Nadine Albert, Jennifer Jackson, Kathy Berger, Ron Trabosh, Pat Dahl, Connie Roberts-Midure, Rosie Kimball, Jon Miller, and Mike Reynolds, all who would stop and ask me how the book was moving along!

I honestly feel that when next year's Merriam-Webster dictionary hits the book stores, right next to the word "Teamwork" should be the words – Lindenwold High School.

As for "Hear Us ROAR!" I will proudly display this book in my office, right on the bookshelf across from my desk. And when I see it, I'll remember your hard work, your dedication, your joy, your sorrow, your heartache, and the genuine passion you displayed for your work. But, most of all, I'll look at your pictures and remember the friendship that those beautiful smiling faces gave to me.

"Too often we underestimate the power of a smile, a kind word, a listening ear, an honest compliment, or the smallest act of caring, all of which have the potential to turn a life around."

Thank you for making so many positive changes in your own lives… for *indeed*; I thank you all for changing mine.

Judith Kristen
December 16, 2006

If you can read this,
thank a teacher.